D0646812

OUR NEW YORK

Text by Alfred Kazin
Photographs by David Finn

1817

Harper & Row, Publishers, New York

Grand Rapids, Philadelphia, St. Louis, San Francisco
London, Singapore, Sydney, Tokyo, Toronto

Grateful acknowledgement is made for permission to reprint excerpts from:

"September 1, 1939." Copyright 1940 by W. H. Auden. Reprinted from *The English Auden: Poems, Essays and Dramatic Writings, 1927–1939*, by W. H. Auden, edited by Edward Mendelson, by permission of Random House, Inc.

"Preludes," from *Collected Poems 1909–1962* by T. S. Eliot. Copyright 1936 by Harcourt Brace Jovanovich, Inc., copyright © 1963, 1964 by T. S. Eliot. Reprinted by permission of Harcourt Brace Jovanovich, Inc., and Faber & Faber.

"by god i want above fourteenth" from *Tulips and Chimneys* by E. E. Cummings, edited by George James Firmage, by permission of Liveright Publishing Corporation. Copyright 1923, 1925, and renewed 1951, 1953 by E. E. Cummings. Copyright © 1973, 1976 by the Trustees for the E. E. Cummings Trust. Copyright © 1973, 1976 by George James Firmage.

"Arrival at the Waldorf," Copyright 1942 by Wallace Stevens. Reprinted from *Collected Poems of Wallace Stevens,* by permission of Alfred A. Knopf.

FIRST EDITION

Designer: Ulrich Ruchti
Associate Designers: Michael Schubert
              Gwen Zazzera

Library of Congress Cataloging-in-Publication Data
Kazin, Alfred, 1915–
    Our New York/text by Alfred Kazin: photographs by David Finn.
—1st ed.
      p.   cm.
    ISBN 0-06-016182-5
    1. New York (N.Y.)—Description—1981-   2. New York
(N.Y.)—Description—1981- —Views.   3. City and town life—
New York (N.Y.)   I. Finn, David, 1921-   II. Title.
F128.55.K38   1989
974.7'1043'0222—dc20   89-45048

89 90 91 92 93 DT/MPC 10 9 8 7 6 5 4 3 2 1

CONTENTS

INTRODUCTION 14

THE FACE OF NEW YORK 17

THE PROMISED CITY 55

THE FREEDOM OF THE CITY 83

COMING OF AGE 127

A CREATIVE TOWN 139

ALONE IN THE CITY 171

POSTSCRIPT:
WE ARE ALL HERE 218

ABOUT THE PHOTOGRAPHS 222

To our New York;
To our grandchildren

INTRODUCTION

Our New York reflects, above all, it contains, the life experience of two New Yorkers who started in Brooklyn, who have New York in their blood and bones, who have lived New York through and through, who owe to New York the freedom of their lives and their very sense of art.

The streets of New York can do a lot for the observant. They developed in us a capacity for attention not far removed from a New Yorker's habitual sense of danger, a love of city detail rooted in the harshness but also the perpetual drama of city life. Above all, they gave each of us— growing up in different circumstances, in very different families, with very different temperaments, aptitudes and gifts for life and art—a hungry sense of the city as our daily resource, the city as home to what is deepest in our sense of existence.

Since boyhood I have made a point of entering in a personal journal my daily experiences of city life in all its familiarity and strangeness, its violence, even its horror not unmixed with the theatricality, absurdity and terrible beauty that New York can show in the most unexpected places. This journal was begun as a literary exercise but became a most urgent need and constant satisfaction. Writing in it has often been as delicious as falling into bed. The journal reflects the passion of a lifetime— watching New York, taking it all in as one walked about, recognizing at every step that one was privileged to be moving, with so many others, on one of the central stages of the modern world. Out of the journal came the practice in writing a very personal prose for the books *A Walker in the City*, *Starting Out in the Thirties* and *New York Jew*. And this went along with a lifetime of writing literary criticism, intellectual and social history.

David Finn, describing himself as another "walker in the city," found his own visual imagination reflected in that book. He thought it "captured in an almost uncanny way precisely what I felt as I walked the city." Riverside Drive (now Riverside Park) and Central Park were his favorite haunts.

The central passions of Finn's artist life turned out to be sculpture and the photography of sculpture. No one else comes close to him as a photographer in this field. It is the ruling sense of pattern and form he brings to his photographs of the city that makes this book so different from the usual frigid shots of "amazing Manhattan" in the usual picture books allegedly about New York.

This passion for the forms released and presented by sculpture led Finn to the myriad forms presented by his native city. He has developed a special eye for the "embrace of life" in it, as he called his first book. Just as his portraits of city people in this book are remarkably composed as well as humane, without tricks and self-dramatizing gestures, so his quiet studies of New York structures never seek to overwhelm us—they are clear-eyed, undemonstrative, naturally positioned photographs that show us what we are used to seeing. But never before have we realized how *present* they are, how much a part of our lives.

If David Finn as artist identified himself with my need as a writer to dig into the sensory life beneath the surface, I discovered in Finn's work, often for the first time, the visual truth of what he had been looking at all his life.

It was this happy concurrence of imagination that brought together for the making of this book two different men pursuing in adult life very different careers. It made for two *authors* of the same book. This is not a text embellished with photographs, or photographs eked out by a text. It is a common enterprise. Many a shot for this book was first suggested by the writer. And the prose owes much to the reflections and sensibility of the artist as we went around the city together—beginning with our early years in the Brownsville section of Brooklyn, so long abandoned and forgotten by the many successful and even distinguished men and women who began there.

Walt Whitman, in his great inscription at the head of *Leaves of Grass,* sang, "One's self I sing, a simple separate person. Yet utter the word Democratic, the word En-Masse." This book, as befits a book about New York by the descendants of immigrants, takes off from "the word Democratic, the word En-Masse." But we have also taken the liberty, as writer and artist, of remaining "simple separate persons." Children of the city, we have sought to bring out from within us our deepest associations with the city that has formed us.

THE FACE OF NEW YORK

*T*he subject was every-
where—that was the beauty,
that was the advantage; it was
thrilling, really, to find oneself
in the presence of a theme to
which everything directly contributed, leaving no touch of
experience irrelevant.

—Henry James on New York,
The American Scene

The daring of New York never diminishes for me as the plane descends to La Guardia or Kennedy through a forest of lights, as I look down and across New York at sunset from the fortieth floor of the Grace Building (my university office!) and see those towers fall into waves, rising and falling. As the Prussian Marshal Blücher said, looking at London from the Tower: "What a city to plunder!" New York the ever-fabulous, New York the spellbinding apex of the technocratic world, offers itself limitlessly to the visual imagination.

"A good place to dream," said Jorge Luis Borges of New York. "I love Buenos Aires, where I live, and London and Paris, but New York is like ancient Rome, the capital of the world." "A catastrophe," said the architect Le Corbusier, "but a beautiful catastrophe." "The supreme metropolis of the present," said the English writer Cyril Connolly, "an unforgettable picture of what a city ought to be: that is, continually insolent and alive. . . . If Paris is the setting for romance, New York is the perfect city in which to get over one, to get over anything. Here the lost *douceur de vivre* is forgotten and the intoxication of living takes its place."

The look of it is exactly what Henry James got when he returned to his native city in 1905 as if returning from the nineteenth century. His genteel old "dusky" New York, what a powerhouse now! Beginning at the harbor (before the railway tunnel was built from New Jersey), he recorded in overflowing amazement—

The aspect the power wears then is indescribable; it is the power of the most eloquent of cities, rejoicing, as with the voice of the morning, in its might, its fortune, its unsurpassable conditions, and imparting to every object and element, to the motion and expression of every floating, hurrying, panting thing, to the throb of ferries and tugs, to the splash of waves and the play of winds and the glint of lights and the shrill of whistles and the quality and authority of breeze-borne cries—all, practically, a diffused, wasted clamour of detonations.

No one coming on *this* New York from the nineteenth century (and, in a sense, most immigrants once did) could help being dazzled, painfully. What many a peasant from Calabria and the Ukraine lacked words for was more than supplied by the great historian and icy patrician Henry Adams, who had long been indifferent to New York:

As he came up the bay again, November 5, 1904, he found the approach more striking than ever—wonderful and like nothing he had ever much cared to see. The outline of the city became frantic in its effort to explain something that defied meaning. Power seemed to have outgrown its servitude and to have asserted its meaning. The cylinder had exploded, and had thrown great masses of stone and steam against the sky. The city had the air and movement of hysteria, and the citizens were crying, in every accent of anger and alarm, that the new forces must at any cost be brought under control. Prosperity never before imagined, power never yet wielded by man, speed never reached by anything but a meteor, had made the world irritable, nervous, querulous, unreasonable and afraid. All New York was demanding . . . a new type of man,—a man with ten times the endurance, energy, will and mind of the old type,—for whom they were ready to pay millions at sight.

Even a native gapes every day at the uproar, the unending show, the unbelievable mixture of peoples, the contrasts of wealth and destitution on almost any street, the unceasing volume of sound, the unlocatable explosions reaching us, as it were, from the "big bang" that started the universe off.

Now that the New York sky is as busy with traffic as the streets, the streets can seem more confining than ever within the profusion of buildings closing in on themselves, a mad geometry of clashing sizes, ages, colors. A maze of upright parallelograms absorbing one another into a collective pattern never intended by the architects, dinosaurs seeking each other's company while the hemmed-in people below are trying to get safely across the streets. The full twentieth century is finally here, as it ends.

Little did the early-century prophets of supercity know that the El would still be darkening parts of the "outlying," the "bedroom," boroughs. Or that in many unprofitable overlooked neighborhoods in this amazing jumble, the nineteenth century, with its old-law tenements, railroad flats, dumbwaiters, fifth-floor walk-ups, has never departed. Side by side with the glitter that Truman Capote adored as "this island, floating in river water like a diamond iceberg," are whole districts, impacted human enclaves, that represent "urban decay" not yet ready for "urban renewal," maybe decades removed from getting "gentrified." Whole neighborhoods in upper Manhattan seem unreal in their broken state as your taxi passes them on the way to the airport. "Don't go in there," a police inspector said laughingly, "without a rifle company."

Yet it is all "fabulous." The fable signifies extraordinary power and will—"the city of ambition," Tom Wolfe calls it—and includes beggary, destitution, homelessness and crime on a scale that astonishes everyone but New Yorkers. Yet the pressures of life and death keep the inhabitants on edge, become something they *wear* as they rise up every morning ready for anything, ready to travel any distance, ready for a subway system guarded by battle police.

And in some way it is all thrilling because of the physical setting that bespeaks the legend of the promised city—the approaches and entrances, the waterways and bridges, the highways and terminals all leading up to the mighty towers that for almost a century have backed up the legend, and that add up to the outsider's image of New York as improbable. Many a foreigner has described the wonder of New York without noticing the people. The image of physical New York in so many photographs, films, sardonic cartoons turns the city into idol, fashion window, futuristic nightmare —*scenery*.

The *face* of New York (which to born and seasoned children of the city like the two authors of this book has never replaced the city itself and its people) may well be the most photographed site in the world. Almost a century ago, when picture postcards first came into view, the then largely New York–based printing industry (long departed from New York) "poured forth a torrent of postcards," says the historian of New York photography Benjamin Blom, "depicting New York as home of the nation's (and the world's) tallest buildings, including the Statue of Liberty."

These postcards fostered the enduring legend of New York as the last word in the long history of metropolis, the megacity, the awesome, the ever "unbelievable." The New York public's characteristic pride in bigness and flair of every sort—even the trials of living in New York—was lifted to the heavens by the completion of the Brooklyn Bridge in 1883; it was so immense and audacious in conception, positively staggering in relation to the low structures on either side of the bridge. Until then New York had been dominated by church steeples.

With the rise of Manhattan's skyscrapers at the beginning of the century, New York became one with modernity, the new century, a seemingly illimitable future. "Old New York," remembered only by descendants of the Dutch and English merchants who had been its patricians, had seemed narrow and stifling to its most gifted sons and daughters. Herman Melville, born in 1819 on Pearl Street near the Battery, actively disliked his native city, left in New York tales like *Pierre* and "Bartleby the Scrivener" images of darkness, restriction and mental tyranny. Only the Battery gave relief to New York in *Moby-Dick,* calling to the sea "all landmen . . . pent up in lath and plaster—tied to counters, nailed to benches, clinched to desks." Henry James, born in 1843 on Washington Place just off the Square, occasionally remembered during his long career in England that he had once been a New Yorker. He then described *his* early New York as a village, positively quaint, when the local "constable" was a friend and Union Square a private park. Edith Wharton, born in 1862 on East Twenty-first Street, was near the end of her life in France to turn back to "Old New York" (a favorite phrase of hers) for her material. What she remembered was a totally smug provincial society and a Manhattan that still gave her the horrors:

. . . mean monotonous streets . . . cursed with its universal chocolate-covered coating of the most hideous stone ever quarried, this cramped horizontal gridiron of a town without towers, porticoes, fountains or perspectives, hide-bound in its deadly uniformity of mean ugliness . . .

The most remarkable thing about New York to distinguished visitors from abroad was the great mass of foreign-born, who with their children were more than half the population and seemed to occupy sinister neighborhoods like the Five Points. Appalled leaders of the city referred to the "dangerous classes." The city had long posed a constant question of its "American" identity, leading to a Chicago witticism that "New York is a foreign city of no known country."

"Only in America" could such a center of international life, hope and art have arisen. In the mists of history there had long gleamed a magic island in the west, a new home and happiness for mankind, the dream of Atlantis brought home. And what could this island *now* be but New York? No utopia certainly, even an uncertain haven, New York with its top load of immigrants, its corruption, its world-daring, "heaven-defying" architecture, was to emerge as a quintessential modern experience.

A superrefined Harvard eminence, Charles Eliot Norton, saw New York from a distance as answering to the need and giving expression "to the life of our immense and miscellaneous democracy." New York must be regarded, never before so much as now, as the most reckless and limitless experiment in democracy.

Spectacular, "unbelievable," forever replacing itself, a living theater whose lights never go out, so formidable to itself as to seem unseizable as a whole, New York's excessiveness in every department of life would have discouraged the great European novelists Balzac, Dickens, Dostoevsky. It has never held any terrors for the photojournalist who pounced to add to the daily havoc with "great shots," "terrific shots" of Manhattan as scenery, blazing away night and day with the great towers as man's only horizon.

We open by dwelling on the city's frontiers—the harbor, the bridges and their approaches, the rivers and expressways, the skyline, the massive walls that New York towers present to the street, the solid slabs of stone, steel and glass marked off yet subtly entwined by the subtlety of their supporting lines—some ornamental, some not.

The fascination of New York to both of us always returns to its coastline, its limits that we see as openings, its borders and bridges. From a helicopter David Finn takes in the ever-startling coast of lower New York, the concentrated world financial and investment centers, tall or squat, hulking over the one level area (still thick with trees) that is the Battery, the twin monoliths of the World Trade Center always in the background. Finn follows this up with loving shots of the harbor's links, the Whitestone and Throgs Neck bridges, the George Washington Bridge—Le Corbusier called it "the only sign of grace in a disordered city"—the openwork steel towers and cable curves that excited the great French architect are right up against our eyes in Finn's close-up. The great thing about the George Washington Bridge is that it always looks so piercingly lean, "elegant," as mathematicians say of its catenary curves all in repose, yet unmistakably tensile as it carries the mighty structure across. In other photographs Finn has caught well the roughness and neglect that surround all approaches, necessary to New York bridges but somehow not *of* them.

Of late nothing has so enhanced the beauty and pleasure of New York at its coastline as Battery Park City. This vast construction, a myriad of buildings in vitally contrasting styles, no doubt brings unexpected sides to *living* New York, seeing so much of it outside your door up and down the Hudson. But what is most unexpected to the outsider is the Esplanade, stretching gloriously along the river, which even in its half-finished state makes New York look and feel a city entirely new. This is the first happy impression walking the Esplanade, which will before long bear inscriptions along the route in tribute to New York and the spirit of freedom from its many writers and foreign pilgrims. The South Cove of Battery Park City is an extraordinarily reposeful spot, and it is nice to learn from the management that "many responses are encouraged. Some benches face inward, some look out over the river, some almost sit on the water." Finn's photograph of the Esplanade conveys a general happiness.

In his images of the coastline, you can see why Manhattan lives between its rivers, not across and *with* them. This makes for river observers, not river walkers. New York is an ocean city, not a town bisected by its rivers like London, Paris, Rome, Florence. It was built up not from the center but from the edge. It built forts to repel invasion from the sea. It was first of all a harbor, a gateway; an imperial prize fought over by European powers, it fell first to the Dutch, then the English.

There are no lovely canals within the city as in Stockholm, Amsterdam, Leningrad, no sweet miniature bridges that the inhabitants walk as continuations of the streets. There are more than two thousand bridges in the New York area; they are for vehicles, not people. Except for the central promenade John Augustus Roebling thoughtfully provided to the Brooklyn Bridge (1883), there is no easy, comfortable, entirely safe passage for pedestrians making their way along the very last pathway next to the water—Suicide Alley! on the Manhattan Bridge, the Williamsburg, the Queens-

boro, the George Washington. The very latest New York superbridge, the Verrazano across the Narrows, of course makes no provision for walkers at all.

For most of New York's people the harbor is not a daily, intimate part of their lives. It is just a view, merely spectacular. In one sense the harbor is now closer to Latin America (as it used to be closer to Europe) than it is to the city's central activities. Just now, the rusted battered crumbling dockside areas along the equally pathetic West Side Highway are one of New York's many eyesores. A few strays contentedly sunning themselves off the splintered boards of a midtown pier cannot make up for the ocean liners that were once lined up, parallel parking, at one pier after another.

For most people, New York is its skyscrapers. A Chicago architect may have been the first to *think* skyscraper, but New York turned it into a product. The skyline became the city's logo: *We* are "the masterpiece of contemporary civilization" (Ada Louise Huxtable). No other city for the greater part of the century has been so immediately recognizable for corporate drive, technical daring and flair, the composition of thrusting, uprearing masses of buildings, one group rising on the wave created by another and still another. New York created skyline as the proof that *any* city in the world, no matter what else surrounds it, can be modern.

Corporate headquarters are our fortresses, and by no means our only ones. They are as mysterious, though accessible, as leveraged buy-outs to the average man. Still, they flatter us. No mean city, this. "We" are the biggest and the richest. The weight of so much wealth is New York's fame and icon. These buildings lean on everyone, visitor or native, by the sheer volume of their self-importance. In the street the bystander can feel pushed around by their bulk. As W. H. Auden wrote of experiencing New York for the first time in "September 1, 1939,"

Into this neutral air
Where blind skyscrapers use
Their full strength to proclaim
The strength of Collective Man
Each language pours its vain
Competitive excuse.

This reaching for the sky above the gridiron of numbered streets and avenues (laid out early in the last century) had a lot to do with the city's sense of style in all departments of life, its proud sense of New York as avant-garde in its daring. It also bespoke the managerial, all-directing boardroom which the rest of New York rarely sees, the cast of mind that first saw itself as a filing cabinet and now as a computer. Cass Gilbert's Woolworth Building (1913), rapturously greeted by a leading clergyman as inspiring "feelings even too deep for tears," was christened by him "the cathedral of commerce." The most distinguished early twentieth-century skyscraper, for decades "the highest building in the world," managed to be as spare and functional looking as Frank Woolworth himself, yet exacted the admiration due its intricate Gothic-impersonating filigree.

Skyscrapers even before William Van Alen's Chrysler Building (1930), the Art Deco masterpiece of a decade, a style that in the true New York light can thrill the eye from a distance as even Mies van der Rohe's Seagram Building (1958) does not, represented a conscious severity that "made" the skyline in midtown.

Has it been noted what abstract pictures the skyline makes? That it probably stimulated Mondrian as an exile in New York to ever-

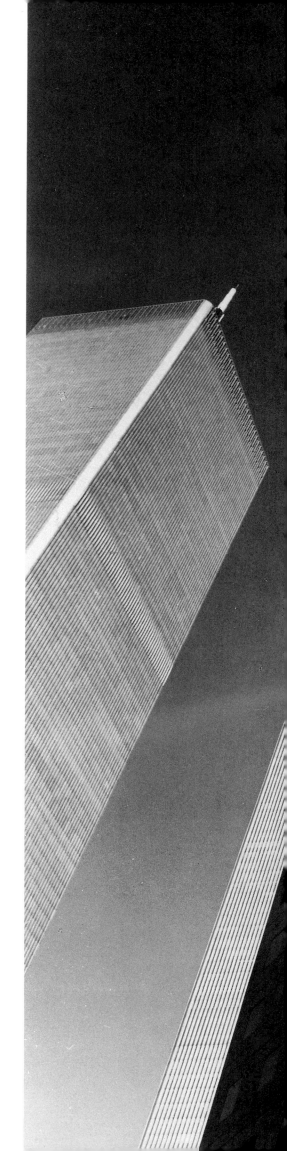

more-autonomous design, and after the war was reflected in abstract expressionism? The many patternings of color were already there in the contrast between the brilliant New York sky and so much artificial light, in the propulsion of so much activity and optimism that made Scott Fitzgerald in the 1920s say that "New York had all the iridescence of the beginning of the world." In the late 1980s, a professional connoisseur of New York, bewailing the power of the developers to dismantle what was ever beautiful and arousing in New York, happily remembered about the outward city that "seen from the harbor at dusk on a summer evening, it leaps up out of the sea as Venice leaps up out of its lilac-colored lagoons."

David Finn's photographs afford us the deepest recognition of our daily environment and thus annul our usual distraction and inattention. The places we use, that we ride, that we pass without thinking of their inherent form and utilitarian beauty. The entwining curves of concrete supporting the Bruckner expressway and curving around each other like lovers. The spires of St. Patrick's Cathedral with the whole structure reflected in the neighboring glass. The striped, boxlike pyramids of the indistinguishable office buildings marching in procession up Sixth Avenue. New York's current street lamps as they swoop and bend like old-fashioned goosenecks, their curvilinear tops perched like party hats on street columns absurdly tall in proportion to the lighted portions themselves. The undersides of bridges, the supporting struts of bridges, the towers, the curves, the swoop and descent of bridges. The intricately decorated glass windows over the door on West Forty-fourth Street of The General Society of Mechanics and Tradesmen of the City of New York Instituted 1785. (The lofty inside hall gives

one more a sense of nineteenth-century space than anything else in midtown.) The travertine walls, just barely tarnished, of Lincoln Center, "a creamy white marble available only from the ancient quarries near Rome." (What a surface to bear the bombardment of New York weather and West Side traffic!) The squat and rotund office buildings rising above the grubby old dockside street, all the way down in lower New York, that once held Sweet's Restaurant, "Charles J. Lake and Lea Lake, Props."

It all comes with knowing how to look. Finn, always alert to the inherent strength of a physical form, what *keeps* it over the years, brings out the subtle lines and springing rhythms of unnoticed city structures, the sometimes awesome mass and body of what has lasted through the years. He has an instinct for pattern and the hidden dynamic that acts as one harmonic act of attention, takes in as one the mass presented to the street by New York skyscrapers and the jauntiness these "too, too solid" structures act out as they reach for the sky.

David Finn catches from the street the unprecedented grouping of skyscraper columns —to his camera eye a merging originally unintended now falls into a Stonehenge of parallels, continuities and divergences. What fascinates me in one shot is the way in which one building closes in on a particular wall next to it so as to interlock the adjoining walls. That daunting look of New York office structures coming right at you! We are surrounded, as human beings totally overmatched. This is New York all right, power city, the American concentrate. Every inch of it costs more than you will ever know. This onlooker is staggered by the thought of how very much goes on behind all those windows that *he* will never know. Whole populations arranged in layers of office boxes, all caught up in most important duties, yet not seeing what *we* see from across the street. Some windows carry darkness as a positive weight, some are all crystalline and staring white from the bars of fluorescence in the ceiling.

The abstract design Finn has extracted from these mighty walls is really formidable. Sheer Mondrian, reproducing the increasing abstractness of office work in New York's corporation headquarters. All thinking here seeks to be strategic in the advance of profit. Nobody here actually *makes* anything. The walls are hung with what is acceptable by the Museum of Modern Art. Everything here is functionally in tune with the latest. As Einstein said, the history of an epoch is the history of its instruments. The shelves are crowded with *tchotchkes,* the bulletin boards with pop art jokes and homemade cartoons. You can't deny the derisive American his

innermost self! But each desk is a wired-up console centered on the electronic screen endlessly serving up numbers and graphics. The equipment is so up-to-the-minute that a stray piece of paper just to *write* on can be hard to find.

All is electric with occupation, with continuous *doing*. Everyone preoccupied with something that absolutely demands his/her presence. The elevator itself hums with the satisfaction of people who expect to be needed. The crowds airily leaving the building after work share a breeziness, are a sort of family. Outside, to the figure in the street who is not included in this collective, just *looking,* the whole structure as it closes in for the night presents a cold voluminousness that turns the onlooker tight with awe. New York at "the violet hour," when the troops descend. A marvel of release, an unending marvel.

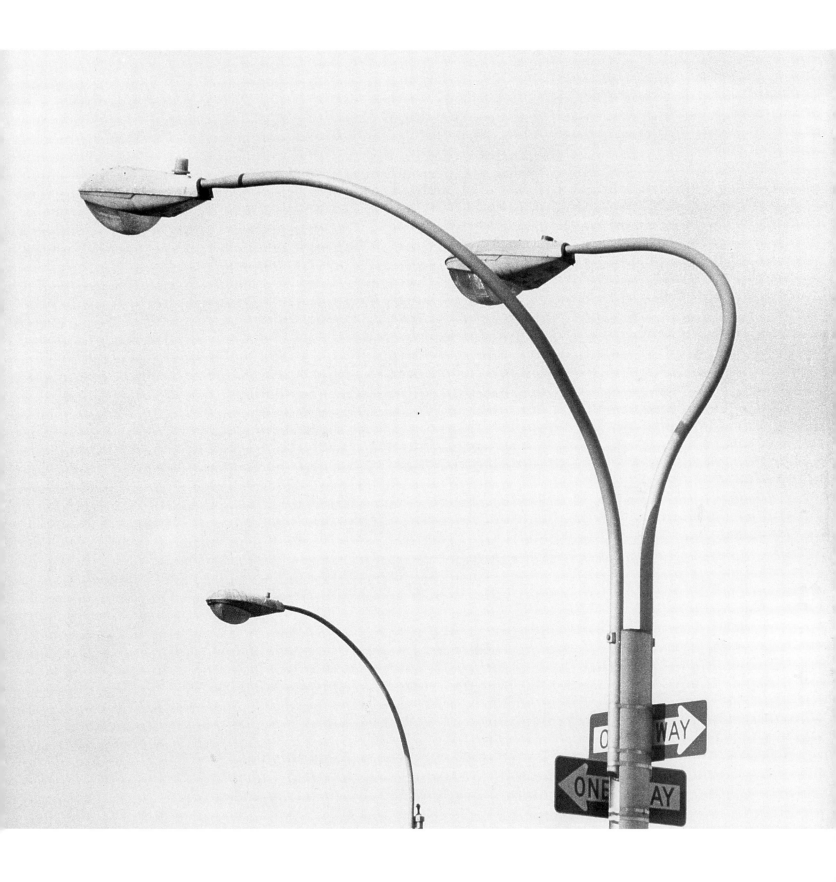

THE PROMISED CITY

One's self I sing,
a simple separate person
Yet utter the word Democratic,
the word En-Masse . . .
Of Life immense in passion,
pulse and power,
Cheerful, for freest action
form'd under the laws divine,

The Modern Man I sing.

—*Walt Whitman*
Leaves of Grass

The first and last thing Americans learned about the place: "It is impossible to live in New York." The most brilliant of southern writers after Faulkner, Flannery O'Connor, began her career with a story about a southerner in New York fiercely attached to a geranium plant that he cannot keep alive. "People boiled out of trains and up steps and over into the streets. They rolled off the street and down steps and into trains—black and white and yellow all mixed up like vegetables in soup. Everything was boiling." The city was "soiled," congested, sloppy, smoky, unruly, smeared over by millions of what Dreiser called *"unsignificant people."*

No doubt he meant foreigners, immigrants. There were Americans like John Reed from Oregon who thrilled to New York in the innocent days before 1917. Lincoln Steffens from California was as fascinated by the ghetto as "other boys were by cowboys and Indians." But more and more, to those who still felt a certain tenderness about "Old New York," the city seemed swamped by Jewish immigrants. Confronted by the Lower East Side in 1905 (he had attended school in Rutgers Square), Henry James was appalled but admitted New York to be "the city of redemption." Still, what a sight:

. . . the intensity of the material picture in the dense Yiddish quarter . . . a great swarming, a swarming that had begun to thicken, infinitely, as soon as we had crossed to the East Side and long before we had got to Rutgers Street. . . . There is no swarming like that of Israel when once Israel has got a start, and the scene here bristled, at every step, with the signs and sounds, immitigable, unmistakable, of a Jewry that had burst all bounds . . . .
The children swarmed above all—here was multiplication with a vengeance; and the number of very old persons, of either sex, was almost equally remarkable . . . using the street for overflow . . .
No district in the world known to the statistician has so many inhabitants to the yard—the scene hummed with the human presence beyond any I had ever faced. . . .
What did it all really come to but that one had seen with one's eyes the New Jerusalem on earth? . . . When I think of the dark, foul, stifling Ghettoes of other remembered cities, I shall think by the same stroke of the city of redemption. . . .

James could not catch the thrill (and fright) of coming straight at the New World by way of New York. "Conjure the contrast between the first sight of Canada and the United States," wrote a distinguished Canadian scholar. "America presented a clear coastline marking the definitive limit of the ocean voyage; suddenly, there was the lush garden of the New World—or the skyline of New York City and its colossal liberty goddess bespeaking the age of reason in which the republic was conceived. But for ships' passengers entering Canada through the Strait of Belle Isle, there was still many days' journey, past the great gulf and up the river, through the savage wilderness to Quebec or Montreal."

Americans in the days when New York was the harbor of harbors to all the world identified the new promise of their lives with the "liberty goddess," mother and protector. America then sang its siren song from the statued "New Colossus" on its very own island. The immortal words on the pediment came from a sonnet by a most genteel spinster from New York's tiny, proud Sephardic enclave, which had arrived more than a century before. Miss Emma Lazarus was a friend of Ralph Waldo Emerson's family in Concord—the first "Jewess" they had ever seen—and a very proper lady not given to unseemly demonstrations of emotion. But she was overcome by the pogroms in Russia after the assassination of Alexander II and wrote the sonnet to show her solidarity with people unknown to her. She could not conceal some slight aversion from those she had Liberty welcome:

Give me your tired, your poor,
Your huddled masses yearning to breathe free,
The wretched refuse of your teeming shore
Send these, the homeless, the tempest-tossed, to
    me:
I lift my lamp beside the golden door.

The golden door! For millennia mankind in the east had dreamed an island in the west, beyond the pillars of Hercules, a magic island where the long-suffering race would get a second chance at life. Eighty years after Emma Lazarus's words went out to all the world from New York harbor, an exhibition, largely of photographs, opened at the Jewish Museum on Fifth Avenue: The Lower East Side, Portal to American Life. Every day saw crowds of obviously prosperous, well-dressed, immensely sophisticated people—the usual museum crowd —standing in front of magnified photographs of their parents and grandparents waiting on Ellis Island benches or tending pushcarts while children got some relief from August in New York by splashing at open hydrants.

The most extraordinary photograph, by Jacob Riis, showed a bearded Jew preparing for the Sabbath—in a coal cellar on Ludlow Street. It is 1900, he lives in the cellar, but there is a Sabbath loaf, *challah,* on the grimy table in front of him, and he will not end up in a Polish ditch for the greater glory of the master race. Almost seventy years later his grandchildren will walk out of that museum, down Fifth Avenue, not even having to say that the city was their America, their savior, that it was once the greatest

frontier known to man. Or as Yehudi Menuhin put it in the darkest days of Hitler's war, "One of the great war aims is to get to New York."

No one has written better about the immigrants' entrance to the city than H. G. Wells in *The Future in America: A Search After Realities* (1906). Unlike his sometime friend Henry James, who was in New York at the same time but had little time for Ellis Island, Wells could not get over what he saw there day after day. It thrills but also subdues me to realize that my parents (who had yet to meet) could have been in the immense crowd:

For the first time in its history this filter of immigrant humanity has proved inadequate to the demand upon it. It was choked, and half a score of gravid liners were lying uncomfortably in the harbor, replete with twenty thousand or so of crude Americans from Ireland and Poland and Italy and Syria and Finland and Albania; men, women, children, dirt and bags together.

The wholesale and multitudinous quality of that place and its work. I made my way with my introduction along white passages and through traps and a score of metal lattices. . . .

The sentences of deportation pronounced in the busy little courts below. . . .

We traversed long refectories, long aisles of tables, and close-packed dormitories with banks of steel mattresses, tier above tier, and galleries and passages innumerable, perplexing intricacy. . . .

A neat apartment lined to the ceiling with little drawers, a card-index of the names and nationalities and significant circumstances of upward of a million and a half of people who have gone on and who are yet liable to recall . . .

The central hall . . . All day long, through an intricate series of metal pens, the long procession files, step by step, bearing bundles and trunks and boxes past this examination and that, past the quick, alert medical officers, the tallymen and the clerks . . . It is a daily procession that, with a yard to each, would stretch over three miles, that any week in the same year would more than equal in numbers that daily procession of the unemployed that is becoming a regular feature of the London winter. . . . What in a century will it all amount to? . . .

On they go, from this pen to that, pen by pen . . . towards a desk and a little metal wicket—the gate of America. Through this metal wicket drips the immigration stream—all day long, every two or three seconds an immigrant, with a valise or bundle, passes the little desk . . . into a new world. . . .

In one record day this month 21,000 immigrants came into the port of New York alone; in one week over 50,000. This year the total will be 1,200,000 souls, pouring in, finding work at once. . . .

As a boy I liked nothing better than crossing back and forth on the Staten Island ferry, the ferries to Hoboken, Weehawken, Jersey City, watching steamers lazily making it up the Hudson to Albany, down the Jersey coast to the Atlantic Highlands. There were boats, boats everywhere—to Coney Island from Forty-second Street, to Boston past Port Judith, to the South. Best of all was the old Dyckman Street ferry that landed you at the foot of the Palisades, ready to hike up to Edgewater.

I never got over my first sight of the Battery, the fire station jutting into the water, the Aquarium in what was once Castle Clinton and is now Castle Clinton again (the fish are at Coney Island). There was nothing in the world like getting on the Staten Island Ferry for a nickel, yelling, "Gangway for Europe!" and hearing the Italian shoeshine man making his way around the decks crying, "Lotsa time! Lotsa time!" But the greatest pleasure, enduring a lifetime, starting from the time as a schoolboy I found myself wandering the great central promenade in amazement at all it enabled me to see of

the harbor and the city *at once,* was Brooklyn Bridge. The story of its making and its maker remains the great New York story.

It took years of walking the bridge, learning its effect on New York, to absorb what the German immigrant John Augustus Roebling desired for the city's people when he wrote in his original prospectus: "This elevated promenade will allow people of leisure and old and young to stroll over the bridge on fine days. I need not state that in a crowded commercial city such a promenade will be of incalculable value."

Roebling was haunted by bridges. The wire rope he invented made a business of the German colony he founded at Saxonburg in western Pennsylvania and was crucial to support the flying bridges that expressed his inventive, scientific and metaphysical mind. It had taken him a long time to get to the "great East River Bridge," as it was first called. Meanwhile he had invented safety devices for portage railways and had taken out patents on inventions to ensure the superior strength and safety of bridges. An original in every way, he found himself perfectly at home in America and became a transcendentalist. What other bridge engineer could have said of himself, "It is a want of my intellectual nature to bring in harmony all that surrounds me. Every new harmony I discovered is to me another messenger of peace, another pledge of my redemption." In his treatise *The Condition of the United States Reviewed by the Higher Law,* he urged his fellow citizens to consider the United States not a business partnership but a family—a "parental estate."

Roebling was from Mühlhausen in what is now Thuringia, grew up in a walled town amid the Gothic churches where Bach had worked a century before. His childhood saturation in Gothic is there for all to see in New York harbor. Two great open stone towers, reflecting Mühlhausen Cathedral, stand in the river like cathedral doors, opening the way to the bay on one side and the river in the other. After his bridges over the Ohio and at Niagara Falls, this was to be his greatest venture. Then, in 1869, while making a preliminary survey for the tower, he was struck by the Fulton Street Ferry as it came into the slip where he was standing. Roebling's death was like something out of classical tragedy written by Ibsen. The master builder was done in by the structure he was working to replace. The author of a thousand-page treatise, *Roebling's Theory of the Universe,* he died horribly from lockjaw. He believed in hydropathy, refused medical attention, never saw his bridge. It was completed in 1883, by his son Washington, who developed caisson disease, "the bends," from working at the bottom of the river preparing the foundations of the Brooklyn tower. Washington sat in a wheelchair at his window overlooking the harbor from Columbia Heights, observing the work through a spyglass, passing instructions to his men through his equally indomitable wife Emily, who shouted them through a megaphone. When completed, the bridge was faithful to his father's original design and his prophecy: "It will be beautiful."

Brooklyn Bridge *is* beautiful in its massiveness, the strength of its towers and its powerful lines, beautiful as the grandest of all connections for the many New York worlds it embodies even as it has survived them. It is so impressive in its charge and flow that it remains New York's venerable center, most cherished tradition, one still in use, and will probably outlive its clumsy and corroded neighbors.

The literature and art created in tribute to Brooklyn Bridge often reflect anxious hopes to see it as the harbinger of a better, visionary America. Yet Brooklyn Bridge is "just" the biggest and best-functioning nineteenth-century structure in New York. To generations of architects, writers, painters, strangers *and* natives still astonished by its power, the towers have represented a glorious adaptation of form to function. The diagonal stays which extend to the main cables from the tops of the towers were devised for safety's sake—Roebling wrapped and fastened his bridge round and round like a trunk. He said the stays would be strong enough to support the roadway if the main cables should be removed.

No one walking Brooklyn Bridge needs to know anything about engineering in order to appreciate the solidity and tension of the diagonal shapes these stays or "suspenders" make as they run from the towers through the roadway. Yet knowledge of Roebling's surpassing technical achievement is somehow forced upon us, as David Finn makes clear in his enveloping views from the river, from the sides, from a distance. There is no better example in this book of Finn's instinct for pattern and form than his view, directly under the Manhattan tower, of the great lines flowing, thrusting, positively *storming* into the tower opening. Yet on every side of these lines are the granite blocks suitable to the year 1875 engraved on the face of the tower, while above it, joined in its way to everything else, is the roadway on which we can see replacements of the gas lamps that once lighted the way. These photographs are quite breathtaking in their grasp of the *inward* composition of forces that make up the bridge. Finn has got to the heart of things here. Yet as always with Roebling's achievement, we are left with the beauty of it all.

Many an American eminence gets into the story of Brooklyn Bridge, from Boss Tweed,

THE LINCOLN
SAVINGS BANK

$2 BILLION
IN ASSETS

who had to be bribed so that a permit would be granted, to the poet Hart Crane, who was inspired to write *The Bridge* when he lived at number 110, Washington Roebling's old house on Columbia Heights. Whitman described the towers going up in his "diary," *Specimen Days*. Henry James in *The American Scene* surrendered to the superenergy radiating from the bridge:

The universal *applied* passion . . . shining unprecedentedly out of the composition . . . the bigness and bravery and insolence . . . of everything that rushed and shrieked; in the air . . . a great frenzied intricate dance . . . performed on the huge watery floor. This organism lacing as by the ceaseless play of an enormous system of steam-shuttles or electric bobbins . . . does perhaps more than anything else to give the pitch of the vision of energy. . . . The monster grows and grows . . . the binding stitches must forever fly further and faster and draw harder; the future complexity of the web, all under the sky and over the sea, becoming thus . . . some colossal set of clockworks, some steel-souled machine-room of brandished arms and hammering fists and opening and closing jaws.

Brooklyn Bridge was first to bring home to Americans after the Civil War the beauty that could be found in industrial structures. Designed in the aftermath of war, a principal force in linking New York's scattered towns and settlements into "Greater New York" (1898), an imperial city, the bridge became to painters and poets—Joseph Stella, John Marin, Hart Crane —a chance to find spirit in so much matter, some "higher" purpose behind the commercial hardness of New York.

New York's best architectural critic, Lewis Mumford, praised Roebling's towers as "the high-water mark of American architecture in the period between the design of the Washington Monument and the last phase of Richard-

son." The poets and painters were less technical but apocalyptic. This was in the Roaring Twenties, when New York led the fashion in literary energy and artistic daring. It was still a great manufacturing center, but led in the printing of books, in galleries and museums. Hart Crane from Ohio, grumbling that he had to write advertising copy for a living, nevertheless got some of his pounding, insistent rhythms from advertising. In *The Bridge* (1930), his would-be epic, Crane frantically tried to turn the famous structure into the royal road leading back into all American history.

This didn't work. What saved the poem was the "Proem," with its overflowing personal longing and entreaty:

O harp and altar, of the fury fused,
(How could mere toil align thy choiring
   strings!)
Terrific threshold of the prophet's pledge,
Prayer of pariah, and the lover's cry,—

To which Crane movingly added the personal confession:

Under thy shadow by the piers I waited
Only in darkness is thy shadow clear . . .
And of the curveship lend a myth to God.

This last line expressed a moving but futile hope.

The bridge is very long, and it is a long, long journey back to where we started from, Brownsville, far from New York in eastern Brooklyn. Of course, we made part of the journey back by subway. This makes for a certain numbing, distractedness, an easy forgetfulness of everything and anything not absolutely necessary to one's safety. For those within the city and new to it, the ever-crowded, always filthy, often-menac-

ing subway in all its bewildering directions represents still another frustration—when it is not just a battlefield.

Finn's photographs of the subway say it all. The subway car, with people helplessly squashed against the doors, looks more damaged, burned out and marked up than a tank blasted in battle. The new cars apparently make the old graffiti impossible, but who can forget SUPER J. BB? Whoever he was, the artist of the curlicues just to the left of the gates between the cars. Practicing art with a spray gun. Norman Mailer wrote a big Think Piece paying homage to graffiti as the work of outlaw artists. Just like Mailer when *he* was the most daring fearless "outlaw" writer. Still, the kids were sneaking into the terminals at night to write some secret message about their lives. But what was it?

The New York subway! Where until recently two different routes on the Independent line were both marked B. Where paint-clotted and barely decipherable maps of the entire system are posted *inside* the moving, jolting train. Where all comfort stations are closed, locked, barred, which may be just as well. Where it is forbidden to make eye contact with the heavy customer jammed against you who is eating a pizza, playing his "ghetto blaster" and standing on your right foot. Where after midnight we huddle together for protection on the platform in a special section marked in yellow. Where the X train, which used to be the Z, really runs "eves Sun after midnight take DeKalb to Destruction."

In the words of Sholem Aleichem: "We did what all Jews do—we came to America. You have to live even if it kills you." And now we are back in Brownsville to look the old place over. I spent my first twenty years in a tenement on the corner of Sutter and Chester. David moved to Manhattan when he was six. He does not remember Brownsville, *all* of it, as I do, but his memories are prouder. His grandfather Rabbi Simon I. Finkelstein, whom my mother worshiped, was the legendary sage of Brownsville from 1902 to 1947 at Congregation Ohav Sholom. When he died just after the war, my parents were among the last Jews hanging on in Brownsville. With East New York and Bedford-Stuyvesant, it was to become the largest, poorest, most desperate black section of the city.

The tenement I grew up in no longer exists, has been replaced by a mound of rubble that to my hungry eye looks like an attempt to obliterate my past. David and I walked up Chester to Pitkin, Brownsville's Fifth Avenue–Broadway–Champs Elysées. On Chester, David photographed what remains of one of the "private houses" that used to line this block. A smart new car is indifferently parked right up on the sidewalk.

Chester Street was once strong in the building of gravestone "monuments." The talismanic word MONUMENTS is all that is left in Finn's photograph. No need to ask what happened to the building itself, or why everything is gone there except the sign still reading MONUMENTS on one side and the name of their maker, one HOLLANDER, on the other. Brownsville is full of wrecks, has for many years looked the supreme New York wreck. Everything down, down, down—the place looks worse than London did after the blitz. Of course Brownsville was always remote, and as Norman Mailer likes to say about Brooklyn, "not the center of anything." Once its very remoteness at the tail end of the city, its many rural spaces and "new" lots, left me the room I

needed to roam in, to be alone in, to dream. Once it was a great Jewish family, thousands on thousands, full of believers, the most obstinate of Jewish believers—though it was not always God you had to believe in. Socialism engaged Jewish toilers and their children as much as did the Everlasting, Blessed Be He.

Brownsville was far away from everything except what mattered to the spirit. The way out of Brownsville was to Eastern Parkway, one of the "parkways" originated by the great Frederick Law Olmsted, creator of Central Park and Prospect Park. Eastern Parkway, with its trees on both sides of the traffic, each tree bearing a memorial plaque to a soldier killed in the "Great War," led straight to the Brooklyn Museum, the Botanic Garden, the central Brooklyn Public Library. So the great world was never far away. And even in Brownsville there was the Glenmore Avenue Library, the favorite oasis of my youth, where we were greeted by six black kids so tickled by the sight of Finn's camera that they kept leaping up and down, shimmying and hamming it up. "Take our picture!" "Take our picture!" As you can see from the photograph, they were in stitches at the sight of us, could not help acting up.

In the empty spaces of Brownsville we laid out our future. Now there are a lot of empty spaces again, but it is the vacancy of breakdown. As the Jews left, the blacks came in, slipping between the cracks. Brownsville is one of the saddest, most derelict, most crime- and violence-ridden neighborhoods in the city.

Twenty-seven-year-old housing police officer Anthony McLean, a three-year veteran of the Housing Authority police force who had received several commendations and citations, was shot to death in one of the two stairwells of a housing project at 340 Dumont. McLean had been searching for a missing ten-year-old girl. McLean was shot during a routine search by the eight-officer housing police task force in the eight-building public housing project, the Samuel J. Tilden houses.

The missing girl, Sheritta Johnson, was found unharmed about six hours after the shooting by an aunt, who discovered that the child had spent the evening with a family acquaintance in a nearby housing project . . . . [She] had last been seen by relatives playing outside her grandmother's apartment at 275 Livonia Avenue.

Black Brownsville extended into Eastern Parkway beginning in the 1960s, and after the usual "racial tensions," as the media calls them, the whites (meaning mostly Jews) moved out. Into *these* empty spaces moved the Lubavitcher Hasidim, the most eager, relentlessly active Hasidic group in spreading Jewish practices among all Jews, like lighting Sabbath candles, studying the Torah and wearing phylacteries, the two small leather boxes containing slips inscribed with scriptural passages and traditionally worn on the left arm and over the forehead by Jewish men during morning weekday prayers.

Who would ever have guessed that 770 Eastern Parkway, the "sacred" office of the Grand Rabbi, Menachem M. Schneerson, would become Mount Zion in New York, and 784–788 Eastern Parkway, filled with Lubavitcher offices and a synagogue, the Jerusalem of the New World? The Hasidic group has offices around the world, from Paris to Honolulu. They have moved in on the tiny communities of Italian Jews, scorning religious practices that happen not to be their own. They regularly accost passersby in New York's midtown, roughly asking, "Are you a Jew?" and if the answer is positive, trying to hustle the fellow into a large Mitzvah Mobile parked on the curb

for a little symbolic practice of the ancient faith.

There are perhaps 20,000 Lubavitcher Hasidim in the Crown Heights section of Eastern Parkway; tens of thousands are scattered around the United States, Israel and other countries. A $23 million new headquarters, a $12 million girls' school on Brooklyn Avenue and a $5 million boys' school on Albany Avenue are in the works, with contributions from David T. Chase, chairman of the board of Chase Enterprises, as well as Jewish investment bankers, and Ronald O. Perelman, chairman of Revlon.

The "Rebbe," Menachem Schneerson, eighty-six years old, holds a title that has been passed down for seven generations from father to son or father to son-in-law. The Rebbe and his late wife had no children, and the question of who will succeed him is officially "not a matter of concern. There is simply no consideration of it." One reason for this is the messianic drive within the movement. Many Lubavitchers see no need for another rebbe because Rabbi Schneerson *is* the Messiah, the anointed leader whose appearance will herald the world's final salvation. A personal aide to the Grand Rabbi explained, "Our sages tell us that the Messiah is a man of flesh and blood who lives among us. In every generation there is a potential Messiah. If I were asked in this generation who was the most suitable, beyond any question in my mind, it would be the Rebbe." Lubavitch has formed a youth group, *Tzivos HaShem,* the Army of God. In recent years the "army" has petitioned the Rebbe to intercede with God to speed the Messiah's coming.

David Finn and I spent some time outside 770 Eastern Parkway looking at the Hasidim. They were reluctant to be photographed, wanted to know if we were Jews, were finally indifferent. I have become very fond of the photograph of

two young Hasidim along Eastern Parkway slouching carelessly against an automobile as if to show their superiority to "progress"—and to us, shaven and hatless.

As usual, Finn is neither hot nor cold, just fraternal and deeply interested. Notice in this photograph the conjunction of these pious fellows' duplicate black fedoras *perched* on the young men's heads with (just to their right) two state-of-the-art garbage cans, one covered and one uncovered. Notice the handsome middle-class brick wall of the nearest house and the stone frames of the windows just beyond the young men. I knew this block when it was most *arriviste,* occupied by ear, nose and throat specialists who charged you a bundle for clearing out your sinuses. The solid lines of trees that Frederick Law Olmsted laid out on both sides of the motorway keep the world, here occupied entirely by the pious, from looking scruffy.

But in this photograph of the two young Hasidim leaning with positive arrogance against the hood of a car, there is an unmistakable suggestion of the orthodox believer's contempt for mere seemliness. Whether it is their car or not, cars don't matter that much to the true believer. This indifference to appearances, an understandable contempt for the secular and sinful world surrounding Eastern Parkway, is shown even more sharply in one young man's very common, multicolored sports jacket and his open collar. This, added to his perching against the car and the one *entirely open* garbage can just to his right, tells us more plainly than anything else how loftily indifferent he is to what the rest of us consider important, perhaps sacred. God and the Rebbe are on his side, and what more can he want? He probably never notices that the garbage can is open. It would not have been there right on the sidewalk, and certainly not wide open, before the Hasidim invaded Eastern Parkway.

The other day I read that hanging over the offices of the Lubavitchers is a large sign in English: WE WANT MOSHIACH (MESSIAH) *NOW.*

THE FREEDOM OF THE CITY

Y ou had such a vision of
the street as the street hardly
understands.

—T. S. Eliot, "Preludes"

One dark winter afternoon when I was fourteen I found myself alone on Brooklyn Bridge after a school excursion to City Hall and the courts of lower New York. In those ancient days the bridge was packed layer to layer, top to bottom, in thundering corridors of parallel traffic. The El growled across it, starting on the Manhattan side from the rusty black terminal that must have been put there not long after the bridge was opened in 1883. At rush hour, when I first met up with the bridge, there was an unstoppable mass of heavy dark overcoats jostling and jamming each other into trolleys and the Elevated trains heading for Brooklyn, naked electric bulbs strung on wires over the open stands whose owners were shouting at you to buy franks, pretzels, picture postcards of the bridge. The bridge seemed to echo the furious blows on each other of all those people struggling to get home.

With evening coming on fast, the dense blackness of everything was shattering. But just ahead of me, the lamps at regular intervals along the central promenade, shaped to fit the original gas mantles, sprang into corollas of flame. I marveled over the fact that high above the river I was walking on wooden planks, many gnashed, splintered and driven apart over the years, so that I could catch glimpses of the iron framework below me and something of the East River. This was long before the engineer David Steinman strung a lower crossway that genuine aficionados (and Steinman, who grew up in sight of it, was a mad lover of the bridge) have never ceased to deplore, charging that it thickens up and blurs the serene curve John Roebling gave his great creation.

I walked steadily ahead in a kind of freezing disbelief at the immensity of New York surrounding me on every side. At the platform built within the arch of the Manhattan tower I stood up against a barrel, held onto the iron railing, and took in New York, all of it at once as it looked to me. On the other side, as I turned my back on Governors Island, were the continuous tenements of the Lower East Side, the electric sign of the *Jewish Daily Forward*—all long ago replaced by housing projects named after liberal heroes and saints—Robert F. Wagner, Alfred E. Smith, Lillian Wald and the *Forward*'s old managing editor Charney Vladeck. But just ahead of me, terraced in solid banks, a great wall opening up where masted ships were still tied up at the foot of South Street, were the towers of New York, a curve of the great skyline.

That unforgotten moment on the observation platform was crucial to me. I recognized the place itself, within the great bridge, as the heartland of New York. In the same moment I knew that the city was more than the material occasion of my life, more than a place of passage. It was father, mother, teacher, the only world I knew so far, a place I had to learn.

The truest sentence Norman Mailer was ever to write: "Brooklyn is not the center of anything." Brownsville, my home place, was even the wrong end of Brooklyn, the end of the line, not too far from the great refuse dumps bordering the ocean at Canarsie. "Can-Na-Sie!" as the vaudeville comics liked to roar out the name in contempt for anything so low and ragged. Brownsville, once all farmland and in my childhood full of empty fields, was home to thousands of Eastern European Jews when the subway finally went out to New Lots. Life was very primitive. Leeches were still featured in pharmacy windows, the sick were still treated,

Russian style, with *bankes,* heated glass "cups" applied to the chest to draw out inflammation. Tenement flats were heated by kitchen stoves and lighted with gas. In the hot summer months horses regularly dropped in the street, and teamsters waiting for the police or the ASPCA to dispose of the horse refreshed themselves in tearooms named Odessa and Roumania. Robbery was common, though not yet Murder, Inc., in the style of Lepke Buchalter and Gurrah Shapiro. Young thieves, playing their parts as if in a silent movie, found it easy to jump from roof to roof just ahead of the police.

My father was a house painter who never knew from week to week how long he had on a job; my mother, a dressmaker, kept us alive during the depression and her two children in college by never leaving the Singer sewing machine. Our kitchen was a dress shop most of the day, with neighborhood women waiting around to consult with my mother over a pattern and to be fitted. My parents were really day laborers, landless and propertyless, living from one piece of work to another. Timid people, absurdly virtuous and idealistic in the old Jewish fashion, given to anxiety as a way of life. They were anxious beyond belief, anxious about everything and anything. My mother looked strained even when she was not bent over the sewing machine, locked up in her body as if in continuous labor. There was no ease to her, no "give," and though she could not have admitted it, little tolerance for those whose temperaments and luck in life were happier than her own.

I cannot recall her ever taking a walk for the pleasure of it, or just reading. She could not read. Nor did I ever hear my parents conversing about anything except the harsh necessities of the week. They were terribly lonely people, with little comfort in each other. My father

reacted to the stiffness of their life by escaping to local union meetings of the Brotherhood of Painters and Decorators and—a great chance for me—by taking me to Manhattan for meetings at the *Forward* building on East Broadway of the Minsker Progressive Branch of the Workmen's Circle. And there was his passion for walking the city, walking anywhere, always looking for a museum, a branch of the public library, an excursion on the Staten Island Ferry, the Dyckman Street ferry to the foot of the Palisades. I was to know many a child of the city like myself, looking to the city for a richer life. My father was the first.

Only in small ways, when pressed beyond endurance, did my parents seem remarkable. My father wept when his hero Eugene Victor Debs died, when Sacco and Vanzetti were electrocuted. At the bottom of the depression, when families unable to pay thirty or forty dollars' rent a month were dumped on the street with all their possessions and people dropped coins into an empty can, my mother thrilled me by leading women to put the furniture back in defiance of the city marshals. The word "city" still meant nothing but authority, the law, punishment and disgrace. Although I always had my nose in a book, I was made to feel that I walked a very thin line, that bad trouble hovered over me like a thundercloud. There was a lot of petty thievery, open graft at the Liberty Avenue police station. Something illicit was always in the air, yet not always locatable. This had something to do with being at the bottom and thinking of resistance all the time.

Not until the thirties and the depression did "big" crime surface with mobsters like Lepke Buchalter. Murder, Inc., was founded to threaten, maim or murder designated victims for a price. But as an associate said, " 'Lepkeleh' loves to hurt people." The gang, engaged mainly in extortion and labor racketeering, was allied in 1932 with Lucky Luciano to form the nation's first crime syndicate. In 1933 Lepke put together his best killer-enforcers, under the command of gunmen Albert Anastasia and Abe "Kid Twist" Reles. Reles, a squealer, "fell" to his death from a window in Coney Island's Half-Moon Hotel in 1941 while guarded by teams of cops. Lepke, Mendy Weiss and Louis Capone were electrocuted in Sing Sing in 1944. These details were to fascinate me because of the occasional presence of Murder, Inc., in Brownsville. Lepke was once pointed out to me in a candy store right on my block. A crowd gathered, cowed but deeply impressed.

David Finn, of a younger generation and a religiously oriented family, was soon whisked off to Manhattan after starting life in Brownsville. Little did I know that when my religiously fearful mother reverently invoked the name "Rov Finkelstein," Rabbi Simon I. Finkelstein, for forty-five years the rabbi of Congregation Ohav Sholom in Brownsville, she was calling for a blessing on the head of—David's grandfather. The Finkelsteins were a great rabbinical family. David's portrait of his uncle, the great rabbi's son, Dr. Louis Finkelstein, rabbi and scholar, shows a very pensive man in old age backed up by holy texts and commentaries so much used that some look positively battered. This is a charming addition to the photograph of his father's tombstone. Rabbi Simon wanted his five published books pictured on the tombstone.

Louis Finkelstein was to become chancellor of the Jewish Theological Seminary, a leader of conservative Judaism in America. He is famous for the meticulous attention to detail in more than a hundred critical investigations of documents fundamental to classical Judaism. When David photographed him, Rabbi Louis Finkelstein, musing about the relations between Jews and other groups in New York, said gently but with unmistakable irony, "They seem to think we're just ethnics."

How differently David and I grew up! I never knew any of my grandparents; David and his family grew up under the canopy, as it were, of a grandfather whose "reputation was legendary." David remembers him as a small man, always with a smile, always cheerful and loving with his grandchildren. One of the rituals when David visited was to play chess with the rabbi. The Rabbi always won. The adults thought David was being nice to him, but it was not so; the rabbi was better. His sermons were spellbinding. In one sermon he said that he was angry at God because of the world's misfortunes. He died at eighty-seven; shortly before he died he wept because he couldn't remember a passage in the Talmud. He had always known it by heart.

The Jews I grew up with had only the most primitive relation to their religious tradition. Just down Chester Street there were two synagogues on the same block, each a separate citadel of orthodoxy named after a different *shtetl* in the old country. No one in "our" synagogue, a moldy old farmhouse named after my mother's village, ever had anything to do with the other. I was not allowed to set foot in it. The lines between them had been drawn for all time. My mother's private devotions moved me without enlightening me in the least. It was not Judaism but the labor movement, with my father's old-fashioned socialism throbbing at the center of it, that made *my* great connection to the outside

Rabbi Louis Finkelstein

world. The cause of labor was international, it was eternally militant and vigilant, it bred great heroes and martyrs. It was as visionary as the primitive church. It *was* a primitive church. To be part of it was to be alive to history. In Brownsville, right on Sackman Street, was the Labor Lyceum, whose auditorium was ringed by a great placard made up of Eugene V. Debs's hallowed words: SO LONG AS THERE IS A WORK-ING CLASS I AM OF IT . . . SO LONG AS THERE IS A SOUL IN PRISON I AM NOT FREE. The next time I saw that placard was in Debs's own house in Terre Haute, Indiana, a local shrine.

Brownsville's Labor Lyceum became famous for more than the cause of labor. Sol Hurok launched his career as an impresario there by persuading the violinist Efrem Zimbalist to perform. Fame being more important than bread, we never got over the fact that at one time or another Brownsville–East New York had been home to Danny Kaye, John Garfield (Julius Garfinkle), I. I. Rabi, Aaron Copland, Meyer Schapiro, Max Weber, and Joseph Hirshhorn, whose great museum in Washington was to be financed by uranium.

My father was crazy about the organizations he belonged to and took me to all his meetings. Nothing in this world, until he became a senior citizen—the only honor he ever received in this life—meant so much to him as a letter from the painters' union addressing him as "Dear Sir and Brother," or the monthly call from the old Socialist Party. There really *was* an American Socialist Party, and nowhere was it more passionately upheld than in Brownsville, which had elected Socialists to the state assembly. Fortunately for me, the most important leaders could be heard only on the other side of the river—in the *Forward* building (long since acquired by a Chinese benevolent association)

and the Rand School on Fifteenth Street.

On Saturday nights, my father leading me clear across Brooklyn by trolley or El to plunge into the bazaar of the Lower East Side, on every street—the East Side of New York, home to all nations!—I experienced what Theodore Dreiser from Indiana called "the color of a great city," what John Reed from Oregon and Lincoln Steffens from California loved about lower New York.

As usual with me, the excitement began with the journey across, the passage over the river. I saw so many church steeples rising above the miles and miles of low roofs that I was back in some long-preserved image of Brooklyn City, provincial and sleepy. A thousand old red fronts and tranquil awnings, streets named Kosciusko, De Kalb, Pulaski, Greene, after generals of the Revolutionary War. Remote "American" Brooklyn, an immense village but still a village to me in those days. Everything was on a scale invincibly local, with "main" streets I was to see again only in small American towns.

Sunday after the war, dreamed Henry Miller from Bushwick in the bittersweet book of that title about going home again. Miller remembered the open-air trolleys of his youth, with people singing along the parallel rows of seats. I remember those trolleys for the long journeys they still made to Coney Island. The conductor had to make his way along the outside platform, holding onto one post after another as he collected his fares, and everybody seemed to know him. There was grass still growing between the tracks as the trolley slowly, slowly, its bell clanging, made its way within sight of the ocean.

Brooklyn is a dream now. We all lived there once, in a world very different from the big city. I was to learn just how different when I went to high school in Bushwick, on Evergreen Avenue, and on my way to school and my favorite branch of the public library, the Saratoga, near Brooklyn's Broadway and the El, passed old German beer gardens that looked as serene as the cafés overlooking the Seine when I saw Paris during the war.

Plunging into the Lower East Side on a busy Saturday night was something else. There were fitfully glittering arc lights along the narrow, darkly huddled streets, jammed along the curb with pushcarts. I could not get over the shrieks and stabs of light against so much darkness, the crowds furiously alive in the street and some long-congealed deadness in the tenements just behind them.

In the twenties and early thirties there were still thousands of Jewish workers, men and women, some children still in their homes. There were painters, carpenters, plasterers, tailors, cloakmakers, pressers, finishers, umbrella makers, underwear makers, leather workers, silk workers, furriers, roofers, plumbers, upholsterers, barrel makers, roofers, bakers, shoemakers. The number and variety of specialty trades never ceased to fascinate me, for as with my mother, there was such a contrast between their delicate skills and the harshness of daily existence. My favorite neighbor was a short squat blacksmith as round and hard as a barrel. I had an uncle who made some of the most sought-after riding clothes in New York. He would have been afraid for his life getting anywhere near a horse.

In their own eyes these workers were proletarians, slaves of labor, exploited. This was a law of life. For all her piety, my mother felt she *lived* the class struggle. If they thought about it, many readers of the *Forward* had no trouble assenting to the call to arms that the paper still published each day in a box on the front page: *"Workers of the World Unite! You Have a World to Win!"* Innocent people, usually without education or much English, patiently enduring the wearing routine of their lives as most immigrants did, they nevertheless believed that their awareness of social crisis made them intellectually more alert than most middle-class Americans. A better world, a wholly different future, was the real business of the working class, and they, even they, were helping to make it.

How did I know this? How did *they* know this? By the force of argument. No young person passing through Union Square Park today (the delightful Greenmarket has pushed out some drug pushers) would believe that the park was once locked in argument all day and long into the night. At my father's various meetings on the East Side nothing so impressed me as the fury with which "comrades" and "fellow workers" devastated each other with words, scorned each other's heresies in the hope—and there always was hope—of showing that one was on the right path to a glorious future. The future itself was not in doubt.

I grew up in a period when the radical passion still dominated the immigrant working class. And what a passion it was! It was a culture, a claim to know the meaning of history past and present, a church, a belief, a way of thinking, a primitive loyalty. Above all, it expressed hope not for oneself alone but for "humanity." And it was all embodied for me in the silent, easily cowed orphan-man, my father, the least impressive man in the world. His father, my grandfather Abraham, an early labor organizer in the garment trades, had died here of lung disease in his twenties. (Many garment workers were afflicted with tuberculosis then and easily carried off.) My grandmother, after bearing his posthumous child, took her children back to Minsk and, after she married again, put my father into an orphan asylum. My father made it back here on his own when he was twenty. One of his laments was that he could never find his father's grave. He couldn't stop wandering the city in search for something, anything that smacked of some larger world. Although he was shy even with me, he took it for granted that I should be at his side.

So there were the rapt early excursions to Van Cortlandt Park at the other end of the subway, to Brighton Beach on the open trolley and delicious Sea Gate, to the Metropolitan Museum in the days when the entrances—both inside the park and to the main hall on Fifth Avenue— were lined with Egyptian statuary, and I sat in the lap of some regally seated pharaoh listening to David Mannes on the balcony overlooking the hall conducting his orchestra. There was Lewisohn Stadium and the Philharmonic in summer, the Brooklyn Museum, the Brooklyn Botanic Garden, the Brooklyn Academy of Music, the second balcony in Carnegie Hall, the free lectures at Cooper Union.

Everything was new then, had the force of revelation, even the great dome of a savings bank as the train swept into Manhattan over the bridge. My father never returned from a Yiddish play without loftily dismissing it as a *shmotte,* a rag. But how he venerated the very look of the grand steps and entrance to the New York Public Library on Forty-second Street (though he would go no farther), the classically draped figures representing Science and Art on the entrance gate to Columbia on Broadway, the gray Gothic buildings of City College.

My father's American culture consisted of official institutions, all the more impressive to someone seated so far from their interiors. One unforgettable evening the Tammany mayor, John F. Hylan, a former streetcar motorman known as "Red Mike," sponsored a performance of *Faust* in Ebbets Field. Even for this we sat in the bleachers. I would never forget my father's rapture when, between acts, His Honor the Mayor, the great man himself, ran up and down the aisles shouting, "Having a good time, folks? Enjoying the show, folks?"

When I was about twelve, the boy on the block who gave me the most trouble, my special enemy in school and after hours, took me aside and said in an unusually confiding tone, "I've discovered the most wonderful poet." "Yeah, who?" "His name is Ezra Pound." It was somehow understood in those days, even among the most vicious handball players on Chester Street, that books were crucial. You had to "know" this and this and that. As Isaac Babel said of his upbringing in Odessa, "You must know everything." People were always testing your knowledge. Though there was a lot of fibbing about what you had read, and how closely, the show of learning forced you to look seriously into some marvelously assorted books. I went every other day into the Glenmore Avenue or the Stone Avenue library for fresh books, and as I returned along Sutter Avenue held up the books so that the titles would impress the boys outside Epstein's candy store. There was always a challenge, some show of bitter competition, in this as in everything else. In books as in handball, life was a battle *mano a mano.*

New York was books, books, books up and down Fourth Avenue in Manhattan, lined with secondhand bookstores from Astor Place to Union Square. In their dusty, shadowy, narrow interiors, books lining every wall from ceiling to floor, books on "special" tables right down the middle of the store and under the awning windows, the owner, the "resident fool" as one described himself, presided over the holy mess as if he were the last possible embodiment of an archaic religion. He too was one of the many teachers, irrepressible culture vultures, whom the irreplaceable city of New York had provided just for my edification.

My "resident fool" was straight out of Mr. Krook's rag and bottle shop in Dickens's *Bleak House.* He had lived so long in the dimness of many books that dimness had taken him over. "A dying trade," he would moan, "this is a dying trade. And I am a fool to stay so long." But he was proud of his dominating bookmanship, a self-educated pedant off the city's streets, encyclopedic in his interests, an inexhaustible pedant who would correct you at every turn. You could hear him any Sunday evening at the Cooper Union lecture series, heckling the professor from Harvard. In his shop he came to life only when you asked for a favorite book of his under the wrong title, or chose what he regarded as an inferior translation of *Crime and Punishment,* or had the nerve to propose delivery of an encyclopedia in seventeen volumes. "For that price you can *shlep* it yourself!"

Year by year I came to identify New York with bookstores, libraries, friendships impulsively entered into for life—so we said—on the basis of a book that had changed our lives. Teachers in high school became friends on the basis of common enthusiasm for a book. Writers I could never meet became friends, the best and most enduring friends one could ever have, because of a scene, a character, a bit of dialogue, that stayed in one's life for years. Writing was *it.* Writing turned the rush, the tumult, the mass fever of New York into an enchantment of recognitions when some favorite book and neigh-

borhood came together. I could never walk down lower Fifth Avenue into Washington Square, past the Brevoort Hotel on the left side of the street, the Rhinelander houses on the right, without thinking of the very *look* of Henry James's *Washington Square* as a book— its thin, dry, utterly luminous pages obviously connected to the Greek Revival houses on the north side of the square.

The site of the old Astor Library (now the Public Theater) on Lafayette Street off Astor Place was real to me because the hero of Abraham Cahan's *Rise of David Levinsky* had spent so much of his time there. The Bowery, with its skid alleys, its salvation parlors, the open markets, the Chinese signs over the remains of old silent movie houses, was still, for all its changes, the world of Stephen Crane's early stories and newspaper sketches of that "depraved" neighborhood. And as you went down and down to the bottom of New York at the Battery, just a turn from where Herman Melville was born on Pearl Street, you were launched into that wonder world of water and far, far horizons that no one captured better than a son of New York at the opening of the most heroic of all great American books:

There now is your insular city of the Manhattoes, belted round by wharves as Indian tales by coral reefs—commerce surrounds it with her surf. Right and left, the streets take you waterward. Its extreme downtown is the battery, where that noble mole is washed by waves, and cooled by breezes, which a few hours previous were out of sight of land. Look at the crowds of water-gazers there.

Circumambulate the city of a dreamy Sabbath afternoon. Go from Corlears Hook to Coenties Slip, and from thence, by Whitehall, northward. What do you see? Posted like silent sentinels all around the town, stand thousands upon thousands of mortal men fixed in ocean reveries.

To find in *Moby-Dick* the name Whitehall, the very one I could see on a pillar in the BMT subway station, made the city doubly mine. To find in Whitman's *Crossing Brooklyn Ferry* the most intimately felt, the most deeply stored images of the harbor bound me all the more to my favorite shorelines on both sides of the river:

It avails not, time nor place—distance avails not,
I am with you, you men and women of a
    generation, or ever so many generations
    hence,
Just as you feel when you look on the river and
    sky, so I felt,
Just as any of you is one of a living crowd, I was
    one of a crowd,
Just as you are refresh'd by the gladness of the
    river and the bright flow, I was refresh'd.

The great thing about the New York pictured in *Leaves of Grass,* anywhere you turned, was openness, horizons opening on every side of you, a sense of community, "the blab of the pave," stagecoaches rolling down Broadway with Whitman next to the driver. The long lines went industriously back and forth loaded with every city sight and sound the omnivorous poet could pack in.

On the river the shadowy group, the big steam-
    tug closely flank'd on each side by the barges,
    the hay-boat, the belated lighter,
On the neighboring shore the fires from the
    foundry chimneys burning high and glaringly
    into the night,
Casting their flicker of black contrasted with
    wild red and yellow light over the tops
    of houses, and down into the clefts of
    streets. . . .

Whitman, "a kosmos," "of Manhattan the son," was sent spinning by the powerful singers he heard in Italian opera at Castle Garden. He would have understood my identifying New York with music as well as writing. With music as a fundamental part of literature because of the "voice." Like most Jewish boys of my generation (Saul Bellow in Montreal, Saul Steinberg of Ramnicul-Sarat in Rumania), I was subjected to the violin at a very early age. The violin dominated the musical imagination in my home even more than Caruso did. The violin was a voice, *our* voice. And of course it was portable, it was associated with *Wunderkinder* like Heifetz and Menuhin who had made their families celebrated and rich along with themselves. The violin was the voice of something deep in Jewish tradition, cantorial, lyric, single, aiming for the heights despite the narrow box from which it sang—yet capable of what fireworks, what ornamentation, what acrobatics!

"Music the combiner," Whitman said. Music meant the velvety splendor of the New York evening even as you trembled from the heights of the topmost balcony in Carnegie Hall so close to the ceiling. It was another world, like nothing else in my experience, and became such a part of me that I seemed to know what I was thinking from the music repeating itself in my head.

Music and, especially, painting were antidotes to the exhausting straightness of Manhattan streets, the gridiron that had been fixed early in the nineteenth century. Exciting as the vistas could be, I longed for a break in the streets, a curve, stairs up a hillside, a colonnade, for a plaza that before Rockefeller Center in the thirties seemed in my boyhood to exist only before the great hotel at the Fifty-ninth Street entrance to Central Park. How unnatural it was, once you climbed out of the subway at Grand Central and fell into the shining greatness at the center of the town, even to look *around* you.

The way was forward and straight up; I was swept into a surge that reached to the top of the highest buildings. Up and down, straight and

across, numbered and ranged against each other
like so many ruled sheets in a ledger, New York
streets carried me in order, with or against my
will, up the stainless steel surfaces of the nearest
skyscrapers, up the steepness of successive stair-
cases, up escalators and humming elevators,
always straight up and across, as if in the same
motion I could climb to the gleaming aluminum
griffins atop the Chrysler Building, the dirigible
mast crowning the Empire State Building, up
and beyond to where invisible sabers lurked in
the icy blueness of the New York sky.

So to walk into Central Park was to
enter a man-made garden contrived to
surprise and delight me at every turn.
From the end of the subway line to this!
To grow up with Central Park as the other side
of life, with the Metropolitan Museum as an
even greater world was to discover a great creation, another world. In the days when it was
unheard of to pack a lunch in anything but a
shoe box, I discovered Egypt, the female body,
the old American scene, and above all Nature. I
wandered off in Central Park from one of these
regulation picnics that took Brooklyn kids to a
May Day festival in the park. I escaped lunch
for Cleopatra's Needle, the Metropolitan
Museum of Art, the Belvedere, the Mall. It was
all so long ago! Boys still wore knickers but-
toned over black stockings. In the sudden freedom of the city that Central Park that day
revealed to me, I walked in amazement among
the mammoth Egyptian statues that in those
days lined both the South Entrance in the park
and the Great Hall off Fifth Avenue. I stared
with beating heart at Degas's breathtaking pas-
tel, *A Woman Having Her Hair Combed*—a nude
just out of her bath, leaning back in the most
luxurious sensual ease, hands on her hips, to

have her great mane of hair combed by a maid.

All around me was the park, a subtle and harmonious country landscape that must have come from God. I did not know that a Connecticut Yankee and true Renaissance man, Frederick Law Olmsted, had planned and designed this wonder, with the help of the professional landscape architect Calvert Vaux, out of a nineteenth-century wasteland of shanties, goats, swamps, bone-boiling factories, to become the first public park of this magnitude in the New World. The rocks, wandering paths, big lakes and little lakes, "rambles" and flourishing gardens were right in the middle of what Henry James, returning to his native city in 1905 and sour on too much democracy like so many New Yorkers in our day, called "the terrible town."

New York was not a "terrible" town to a boy in the Metropolitan's American Wing staring through a few strategically placed windows at May Day outside. The wing was lined with grandfather clocks, portraits of colonial merchants and divines. But there were also pictures of New York sometime after the Civil War—skaters in Central Park, a red muffler flying in the wind; crowds moving round and round Union Square Park; horsecars charging between the brownstones of lower Fifth Avenue at dusk. In the rooms strictly devoted to American painting there was Winslow Homer's dark oblong of Union soldiers making camp in the rain, Thomas Eakins's solitary sculler on the Schuylkill, and most wonderful to me then, John Sloan's picture of a young girl standing in the wind on the deck of a New York ferryboat looking out to the water.

I did not know I loved New York, I did not know there was a New York to love, until I saw it in museums. In the days when all New York bridges were still open to pedestrians, when you could make your way across the great central promenade of Brooklyn Bridge without being mugged, when nothing was such a gift as the light over the East River bursting into a BMT car and breaking up the boredom, I could suddenly make my way between New York and home with the feeling that these halves of my life were joined not by ceaseless daily travel but by images drawn from New York paintings. The struggle for existence made everything else seem trivial, unworthy. The city fell on me every day like so much rain, but I was falling into the subtler impressions it was making. Why was the dome of a certain savings bank—it bulked on the horizon like a cathedral as the subway moved into the open across Manhattan Bridge—so dramatic? Why, long before I knew the photographs of Alfred Stieglitz and Walker Evans, Joseph Stella's clotted Brooklyn Bridge portraits, did the absolute reality of everything they saw in New York streets and approaches haunt me?

New York painters and artist-photographers seemed to love the city more than New York writers did. Some were as romantically tuned into the passing show as fashion photographers. Fondly colored impressions of the crowds at rush hour under the old El. Brownstones and the old, low, red-brick storefronts. Decorative stone, wire, glass whose actual weight in the city had always hit me like a blow. The rooftops exactly like those where the toughies in my neighborhood trained racing pigeons, and where undernourished Jewish featherweights sparred on the gravel before they went out to Canarsie to get beaten. The air shafts and chimney pots so like our own, but sweetly overlooking what I knew as the subway huddle, the heat, the screams in the streets when city marshals threw the furniture out during an eviction.

New York painters brought my chaotic secret impressions into the light. Of course these middle-class painters bravely facing the commonplace and the ugly and getting called the ashcan school would be as sentimental about the city as our earliest painters were about mountains. They thought the grim cheap-dress emporium, Klein's on Union Square, was so pictureworthy that it was almost beautiful. My favorite memory of Klein's remains a crude drawing just inside the store of a weeping girl behind bars, bearing the caption, "Don't Bring Disgrace to Your Family by Shoplifting!" I was amused by Reginald Marsh's bouncy ballets of shoppers along Fourteenth Street. Someone had actually painted Fourteenth Street instead of just barely surviving it—as my father did when, at his local of the Brotherhood of Painters and Decorators, he once in his life voted against the union despot who sometimes placed a revolver on the ballot box—a charmer known even to his family as "Jake the Bum."

The greatest image of New York for me in painting was Edward Hopper's *Early Sunday Morning*. I know now that Hopper did not call it that, but I could see why the absolute silence of the street would lead people to think of Sunday morning—in certain parts of New York. I could not get over the *depth* with which Hopper saw the hydrant, the barber pole, the row of low red-brick houses on lower Seventh Avenue. The bulk of those humanless houses riveted me, finally showed me what an unseen watcher of such houses had for so long seen in them. Hopper could not rest with his own amazement at total silence on lower Seventh Avenue. He had to put that silence back into the hydrant, the barber pole, the low-lying bulk of that dark red row of houses.

For years after the war, walking every day past a certain stretch of dark red houses on Fulton Street in Brooklyn Heights, I was convinced that here and nowhere else was the street wrapped in early morning shadows that Hopper had painted. Even when I learned that Hopper had found his subject on lower Seventh Avenue, I claimed his wonderfully strong, concentrated mass of New York silence for Brooklyn and myself. *Early Sunday Morning* convinced me that there can be telepathy between a picture and the viewer. The passage from Hopper's street to my mind moved me more than any other image of New York. It was the silence that got me— the silence that a painter and even a writer, an unseen watcher, will live in for years—not even knowing all that he is thinking about when he is alone with a street.

But then there was Degas's *Woman Having Her Hair Combed* being stared at in exultation by a boy in long, scratchy black stockings. The shameless down-to-earth woman leaned back in absolute satisfaction, her breasts luminous and tangible against the green of her chaise longue and the red in her hair. Obviously I had made my way not just to Central Park but to someone's inner paradise. Nothing after that could have been startling except the lineup in the Great Hall of Egyptian gods and goddesses with capacious laps that practically invited a kid to climb up and sit in them.

What has never ended for me in Central Park is the spell of Egypt, of so many monumental, ancient and eternally distracted figures right in the middle of New York. Whenever I pass down Fifth Avenue at night and see the enormous glass hangar that encloses the Temple of Dendur, I am slightly oppressed by the enigmatic heaviness of Egypt. Egypt in New York regularly overcomes me by its bulk and proud royal stiffness, remains a mystery because of the unstoppable brooding on death that I saw first in those faces. And then the total surprise of the obelisk, Cleopatra's Needle, from ancient Heliopolis (now the site of Cairo's airport!). That obelisk just across from the red-walled, original park entrance to the museum once stood before the temple of Ra, the sun god: "Atmun, whom the mistress of Heliopolis bore to him, Thutmose, whom they created in the temple in the beauty of their members, knowing that he would exercise kingship through eternity."

Once upon a time the museum, and everything in Central Park surrounding the museum, had the magic of distance to it. The distance was in time—Egypt was even older than the Puritan household recreated in the American Wing! The distance was in space, style, tone. The artful, totally arranged and even manufactured landscape called Central Park, as I learned over the years to recognize Olmsted's cunning hand, was for a long time dazzling but unreal. I felt that I was not so much going into a park as entering a picture.

Whitman complained that the design was suited mostly to New York's elite. Fifteen miles of perfect roads and bridle paths would attract mainly the "carriage-riding classes," "the full oceanic tide of New York's wealth and gentility." And in fact the brilliantly decorative paintings of the park by Maurice Prendergast were paintings of the upper-class scene: carriages, top hats, footmen, ladies with veils. The picture effect was just what the ingenious but romantically inspired Olmsted wanted for "his" park. The park was to be not just a refuge from New York's pressure, relief from the monotony of

the grid, but a thing of positive beauty that should induce the proper reflections in the face of so much "nature." The park, Olmsted quietly boasted, was a "creation." "I shall venture to assume to myself the title of artist," he wrote. "The main object and justification is simply to produce a certain influence in the minds of the people and to make life in the city healthier and happier."

Now that I live so near the park that I can walk right into it and around the reservoir any afternoon, the park is no longer a "picture." It is so busy and packed, relentlessly athletic even at night for joggers (but in packs), so much used, misused and regularly vandalized, that it seems less a "park" than a crosstown artery for traffic, a weather station, zoos, running tracks and athletic fields, a Shakespeare theater, a cottage marionette theater, a place for demonstrations, a skating rink, playgrounds, and a colony for the imperial Metropolitan, which obviously looks down on the graffiti, the dirt and the unruly natives huddling around it.

David Finn has caught without irony the total relaxation and even slovenliness that Central Park now invites. The park could also be called just now the revolt of the masses. Some take off most of their clothes; some, like the figure in hat, beads, shades, long hair and absolutely virile mustache, see the park as a chance to adopt a public personality. The one boy and three girls, the group somehow centered around the beer can that one girl is bringing forth, are seen against an overflowing trash can in the middle and another great whale of a rock on the hillside. The young boy and two older girls on the lake, the great staircase leading down to the Bethesda fountain in the background, seem in the traditional way to be fumbling with the oars divided between them. The young need to be in groups. But how well Finn has caught the bosky look of the park when there are no figures in this landscape, the lovely tunnels that still scare and thrill kids yelling their way through them to raise echoes. Before the many joggers running together at night made the park safer than it used to be, a friend of mine actually walked through it at an hour of night when no one who meant to go on living was likely to be in the park, alone or not. He admitted that nothing whatever had happened to him; it was just a bit lonely. Then he burst out, "It's *my* park and no one is going to keep me out of it!"

Olmsted's ideal consumer of "his" park was probably a fully dressed "pedestrian" with hat and walking stick taking a "ramble" and having, in the spirit of Wordsworth, "elevated thoughts." What you see in Finn's photographs of totally relaxed girls in beach attire huddling together is the omnipresent fact—the young are interested only in each other, couldn't care less for their "natural surroundings," and are "consumers," all right. Of the park itself, which they use and use up as if they were devouring every inch of rock and grass in the interests of what has replaced Olmsted's Victorian idea of the park as place for meditation—total "relaxation."

If you want to know how much *everyone* thinks of the limited park space as a private turf, listen to Peggy Guggenheim in her *Out of This Century: Memoirs of an Art Addict*. Her uncle Solomon's museum at Eighty-eighth and Fifth "is built on a site that is inadequate to its size and looks very cramped, suffering from its nearness to adjacent buildings. It should have been placed on a hill in the park. It is on the wrong side of Fifth Avenue."

When General Grant died in 1885, they wanted to plant *him* on a hill in the park. Olmsted managed to resist that. Olmsted was sure that people needed nothing but scenery to look at; he opposed most of the statues lining the Mall. His park got away from him. By now the park is a "refuge" from the city but what Henry James—this was 1905!—saw as "the singular and beautiful but almost crushing mission that has been laid on an effect of time, upon this limited territory, which has risen to the occasion, from the first, so consistently and bravely." The people, yes. The place looks *inserted* into the city's incessant rush. It needs endless care. With tremendous effort, vigilance, money, it is kept up not just by tax funds but by so many philanthropists and volunteer groups that you might think it was a hospital. During the 1980 transit strike it was marvelously bracing to make your way through the park early in the morning as thousands walked, bicycled and roller-skated through it. Cops all over the place directing this mass pedestrian traffic made it truly seem what the parks commissioner of the time loftily called the "people park." Crime in the park decreased dramatically. In "normal" times cops have been reluctant to get out of their squad cars; "rangers" in Smokey the Bear hats do what they can to keep order.

The park, designed at the high point of Victorian romanticism and upper-class self-satisfaction, full of sites meant to be *looked* at so that your soul will be refreshed, now betrays its artificiality. The open spaces can be a battleground. The lurking little paths can be booby traps. But this is New York as the violent century rushes to its end, with the park bearing every burden of overcrowding and Third World resentment, of athleticism, of the frustrated energy that spurts up in great cities when you are constantly

pushed by crowds and wonder where they are taking you. The park is a pacemaker for New York's straining heart, not a retreat. How else could it be? Here are lakes where there were no lakes, rocks so blitzed out of the New York schist that they look like Henry Moore sculptures. Here is a "pergola" designed to look rustic at the corner of Central Park West and Seventy-second Street, just across from where John Lennon was killed. It now looks as archaic as an outhouse. Here is a "rambles" laid out for breathing in nature with appropriate quotations from Wordsworth, but along whose bosky retreats and curvaceous paths homosexuals regularly getting together are assaulted by self-righteous teenagers from Jersey City with baseball bats.

Joggers around the reservoir, joggers in the rain, joggers darting in and out of traffic, joggers with faces so taut they might be flagellants flogging themselves toward a finish line known only to God. The pursuit of health has replaced the pursuit of happiness. The park has served up cricket grounds for Jamaicans, a rugby field for Britishers, soccer for Latin Americans, ice skating in the Wollman Rink, lacrosse and field hockey, baseball diamonds at every turn, a roller-skating rink and of course endless paths of roller skaters replete with knee guards, crash helmets and radio earphones to keep boredom away. George Plimpton, that indispensable guide to the fashionable life, reports that he has seen *bicycle* polo in the park. Even if Olmsted had lived long enough to see an upper crust in New York composed of inside traders, television producers and nonextraditable Bolivian cocaine merchants, he would not have been amused to see the "croquet elite," as the *Times* calls them, in dinner jackets and sneakers on their own "croquet green," a site described as "a

swath of lush emerald lawn trimmed with red begonias and blue ageratum."

If you do not jog, the masses of hard-breathing people furiously dashing around the reservoir make it difficult for a mere walker even to get out of their way. The joggers are fascinating, however, when they move like dancers; it is startling to witness sexual character and rhythm in the way people run. I miss the old solitude around the reservoir, where one could just walk and walk and watch the herring gulls feeding on whatever it is they mysteriously find along the great pipes in the water.

I once put in a lot of time walking the reservoir, looking at those towering apartment houses that at night, when your taxi enters the park's circular driveway, are so dramatically New York. I walked the reservoir so much because I was madly in love with a girl who never looked so compelling as when we walked the reservoir. Our little time together—it was a wartime romance—coincided with Christmas 1943. The cold New York light did great things for her hazel-green eyes and sculptured dancer's body as we restlessly paced the path. I felt guilty about her, for she was breaking up my life. The thousands of windows surrounding us looked to me like staring eyes. We seemed to be center stage on that hilltop smack in the middle of the city. What a drama it was to be alone with her on that deserted path. I shivered not only in the December cold, but in a passion for her that was being watched by so much of Manhattan.

Seen from a distance, seen from up high, New York enclosing the park looks white, boldly inquisitive. On Fifth Avenue the blocks of white and off-white apartment houses still look new. By contrast, the long blocks of massive apartment houses on Central Park West, looking down to Fifty-ninth Street and Columbus Circle, still seem darkly, solidly bourgeois in a professional way, with a liberality of space necessary to doctors of every description and New York psychodramas unfolding in their many rooms. And what a parade of names to those castles on CPW: the El Dorado, the San Remo, the White House, the Kenilworth, the Ardsley, the Beresford, the Dakota, the Orwell. Once the doormen in their starched wing collars and white dickeys made me think of aged retainers in the House of Lords. These old apartment houses, many of them built so early in the century that they now, like the Dakota, belong to the last, ornamented and turreted like nothing in the gleamingly shallow new Fifth Avenue houses across the park, were built to *last*. And though CPW—the nearer you get to Columbus Circle—is also famous for its show-biz residents, you cannot just *look* at the Dakota, with its gables, turrets, towers, green roofs, its battlements and the windows of maids' rooms just under the gables, without thinking—as I have all my life—that to live there must be a career in itself.

It is a beautiful day at the beginning of May, and I am in my favorite piece of the park: between the entrances at Fifty-ninth Street off Columbus Circle and Fifth Avenue that have always been for me the perfect New York crossroads. The inescapable straight-on of too-regular streets gets some relief here. The entrances to the park—Central Park South with all those artists' windows—are alive and bracing. There is nothing in midtown that compares

for real mixing and endless surprise to the Fifty-ninth Street entrances to the park. Anyone who gets tired of this is tired of life. Now that they have repaired and cleaned the monument to the sailors blown up with the U.S.S. *Maine*—BY FATE UNWARNED IN DEATH UNAFRAID—the statue and the space before it make a perfect platform for revivalists, rock bands looking for an agent, political weirdos, stand-up comedians. I am always afraid to find graffiti on the monument, but some of the characters perched on it actually look as if they were protecting it. This is the only New York rival to the great London spectacles at Hyde Park Corner and Marble Arch.

It is the crossing of lives that I never get tired of at Fifty-ninth Street. There is even a touch of Paris in the roof of the Plaza Hotel, a touch of Europe's once royal parks in the openings on every side, to the zoo, to Fifth Avenue, a touch of long-needed frivolity in the dancing figure over the Pulitzer Fountain. Scott and Zelda Fitzgerald are supposed to have clambered into the fountain one fine drunken afternoon in the golden twenties. The twenties, the great "plaza" itself open to all New York, the horse carriages, the young females and leftover top-hatted geezers who drive these genteel-looking wrecks of carriages with horses much much too patient for the rest of New York, the great St.-Gaudens statue of General William Tecumseh Sherman in his cape and on his horse. What style, friends! An age passed this way, and at times seems here still. This is New York at its best, crowded to the sky, but New York with an air, and looking grand.

COMING OF AGE

Home from Guatemala, back at the Waldorf. This arrival in the wild country of the soul. All approaches gone, being completely there. . . .

—*Wallace Stevens*
"Arrival at the Waldorf"

It is true that one can live and die unseen in New York, but one is also left alone to see what there is to see, to invent to one's heart's content. The more massive and seemingly inaccessible the urban fortress becomes, the more imaginative space within. Resistance is just part of it.

Perhaps the artist is never really "alone." Hemingway, who, as he became more famous and more pompous, seems to have identified New York with the gossip columnists taking down his every manly jest at Toots Shor's saloon, liked to say that New York writers lived like rats in the same barrel. Writers are more solitary than painters, musicians, theater people. But a writer in New York depends on a tradition whether he knows it or not. Greenwich Village long ago became a tourist trap. The days are long gone since a single boardinghouse in Washington Square gave refuge (at various times) to Theodore Dreiser, Eugene O'Neill, Willa Cather, John Reed, John Dos Passos and a dozen other writers. But in the Village one somehow still understands—it is in the air— what E. E. Cummings from Patchin Place meant when he wrote in *XLI Poems* (1925):

by god I want above fourteenth
fifth's deep purring biceps, the mystic screech
of Broadway, the trivial stink of rich
frail firm asinine life

And why John Dos Passos in *The Best Times* (1966) remembered New York as *the* town in which to be a young writer. "There is a time in a man's life when every evening is a prelude. Toward 5 o'clock the air begins to tingle. It's tonight if you drink enough, talk enough, walk far enough, that the train of magical events will begin."

It was in New York that modern literature, modern painting, modern photography, came of age for Americans. John Butler Yeats (the poet's father—Ireland was too small to hold them both) announced in 1912, "The fiddles are tuning as it were all over America." He knew this from living in Chelsea and dining many an evening at Petipas's on West Twenty-ninth Street with Van Wyck Brooks and John Sloan. Before *Seven Arts* magazine died in what Dos Passos called (to the end of his life) "Mr. Wilson's War," it was the most natural thing, this being New York, for Van Wyck Brooks in *Seven Arts* to propose that the slogan of the modern movement be "a warm, humane, concerted and more or less revolutionary protest against whatever incubuses of crabbed age, paralysis, tyranny, stupidity, sloth, commercialism, lay most heavily upon the people's life." "More or less revolutionary" remains the badge of all those from elsewhere gripped by the powerful atmosphere of New York—Willa Cather from Nebraska, Van Wyck Brooks from a "Wall Street suburb" in New Jersey, John Reed the sheriff's son from Portland so proud of being able to write home, "Within a block of my house was all the adventure in the world; within a mile was every foreign country."

There was to be a continued invasion and discovery after the war—Eugene O'Neill and Edmund Wilson in Eighth Street, Willa Cather in Bank Street, Theodore Dreiser in the Ansonia on upper Broadway, Hart Crane, Marianne Moore and Thomas Wolfe in Brooklyn, García Lorca at Columbia. New York was *the* place for any novelist, poet, dramatist, critic willing to challenge it. The battle was not always *mano a mano* in the style of Thomas Wolfe or Balzac's Eugène de Rastignac promising to "take" Paris. Willa Cather lived successively on Bank Street and Park Avenue without anyone (except the very young Truman Capote in the Society

Library on Seventy-ninth Street) meeting her. Katherine Anne Porter: "I never knew her, never met anyone who knew her." But such independence—though practiced in out-of-the-way Queens by the fabricator of marvelous boxes, Joseph Cornell—was rare enough among the increasing number of writers enlisted by magazines with some intellectual pretension. This entailed a very different life from that possible to book writers. As Cyril Connolly said of literary journalism, you get praised on the head, paid on the head. Nowhere since Paris during the Revolution had there been so many visionaries, would-be revolutionaries and fanatics, dialecticians, arcane and angry thinkers, arguments and voices sufficient to themselves, as in New York. Recalling his youth in Brooklyn, Bernard Malamud once said, "I was forever wandering the streets looking for my future." New York gave one a chance to do that.

The people I soon came to know best in New York all led lives separate from their visible selves. They led it crushingly in their heads, like Miss Lonelyhearts in Nathanael West's novel of the same name and the boy in Henry Roth's *Call It Sleep*. Oddly enough, such distracted folk included teachers—in my day the best of them tended to be so inflamed by literature, they could not do enough for a boy already a slave to the written word. As teachers they were too grand to possess first names. But "Miss Harrington," "Mr. Zisowitz," "Mr. Aronson," how excited you got "doing" the great English poems in Palgrave's *Golden Treasury,* and how you kindled at a real exchange with a student about words that more than anything else in the world could raise so many echoes in the human heart:

Fade far away, dissolve, and quite forget
What thou amongst the leaves hast never
  known.

The most vivid people I was ever to know in New York, generation after generation, were those Nietzsche called "argonauts of the ideal," people somehow ablaze, in the midst of their accustomed tasks, to find the "undiscovered country" where, for once, spiritual exiles like themselves, perpetual strangers, could for once feel at home. There was something about New York that drove people to the "end" in everything—painters to work a canvas into some ultimate definition of art, writers to make their work an exception to everyday existence, arguments about the just society that led to irreversible extremes of personal bitterness. For the most creative people I was ever to know, New York was the country of the greatest personal expansion and hope, but also a place of perpetual crisis. Perhaps because there were so many people like oneself, mirroring one's most intimate moods, one's daily gains and failures.

At the peak of his success, wealth, international fame, the painter Mark Rothko stood on the steps of his elegant townhouse in the East Nineties, escaping the party going on in his own house. Framed in its light, the merriment at his back, he talked to me of the consolation he found in Shakespeare's tragedies for the grief he was just now feeling. The usual cigarette burned away in one corner of his mouth (with Rothko everything turned into cigarettes.) The large, very round lenses of his glasses glimmered in the light of the street as if he wore them as a mask. Rothko loved to talk—to narrate and explain—rather than to converse. Once, when he was on an ocean liner returning from Europe and feeling more alone than usual, he went up to a stranger at the bar and demanded, "Let's talk!"

Rothko's stories were rooted in explosive situations, as comic as they were grotesque. A native of Dvinsk in Russia, whose family had taken him all the way to Portland, Oregon, he was actually at Yale for a brief period, not yet fully aware of himself as an artist, an idealistic radical with thoughts of becoming a labor leader. He hitchhiked from New Haven to Portland between terms. Some highways were amazingly bare during the depression despite the migrants looking for work. Once a farmer's very slow and beaten truck stopped for him. To Rothko's great amusement the farmer announced, "I seen you a long way off and said to meself, 'That's a Jew! He may rob me but he won't beat me.' Get in!"

Rothko, like my other "argonauts," had this way of looking at himself from a long way off, of seeing himself as a special case, the end and extremity of something other. There was to be death in this, the desolating sense of having reached a limit in his very body beyond which there was nowhere to go. But black, even mournful, grief-laden as his work became in the years before his end, it was this very sense of an ending that made him go beyond the limits other people prescribed for themselves and everyone else.

As a painter in the postwar mode, abstract expressionism, *very* abstract indeed, Rothko easily came down to the bone, to the frame, to the skeletal appearance of absolute closure. But this series of rectangles swam away from each other in a mysterious atmospheric space that haunted Rothko—the suggestion of a finiteness finding its own deliverance in colors that swooned and floated past each other. Nothing was so tight and yet so free. Rothko could find his own deliverance in the idea of a boundary set by his imagination alone. So the boundary had to recede farther and farther into the magic of space, the indeterminate that all the while,

within so many self-created boundaries, expressed Rothko's nostalgia for the infinite. He was to reach higher and wider, toward an immensity on canvas, one eleven by fifteen feet, that took over the chapel in Houston that became the Rothko Chapel.

What moved me most in gloomily excited Rothko was his way of identifying himself finally with misanthropy and sorrow. In his painting he did try to leave all personal damage behind. In a period after the war, long after, when so many gifted people seemed to themselves to be the most in danger—who can ever say why?—Rothko did terrible violence to himself, hacking clumsily at his body as he never did in his work. But in his work, blacker though the outer frames became, the colors were in constant movement, shifting within and out of themselves, making for the illumination of pure spirit.

Another such influence on me, but beginning earlier, and stemming from his work rather than himself, was Lewis Mumford. When I first came upon *The Story of Utopias,* Mumford's first book, in the school library, I somehow knew what the man was like and where the reach of his mind would take him—to rebuild the city as a community. Mumford, whose great subject was to be the city in every one of its manifestations, was to describe himself as a child of the city. The illegitimate only child of a boardinghouse keeper of German Protestant ancestry, he did not know until he was forty-seven that he was the son of a Jewish business-man with whom she had had a brief affair while she was a housekeeper in the home of this young man's uncle, the man she really loved. At nine or ten Mumford experimented with wire-less radio sets, dreamed of becoming an electri-cal engineer. While at Stuyvesant High School,

which specialized in science and mathematics, he published his first professional articles in electrical magazines and acquired the lifelong interest in technology that was to make him the most famous architecture critic of his day and the future author of *Technics and Civilization* and *The Myth of the Machine*.

Mumford went briefly to City College, withdrew because of delicate health (as this is written he is in his ninety-fourth year), and as he has often said, threw himself upon the city for the rest of his upbringing and education. He was an indefatigable walker, a seeker, a sketcher of city scenes and places who could soon claim all of New York for his own, from the Flushing (then a village) where he was born to the Upper West Side where he spent much of his youth. He knew the New York of backyards surrounded by high wooden fences, when paved paths were too uneven to encourage even tricycle riding, when there was still a "Gas House District." From Sixty-fifth Street up, Broadway was full of vacant lots, "with visible chickens and market gardens, genuine beer gardens like Unter den Linden, and even more rural areas. Since for the first quarter of a century of my life I lived between Central Park and Riverside Drive, wide lawns and tree-lined promenades are inseparable in my mind from the design of every great city; for what London, Paris, and Rome boasted, New York then possessed. . . . "

Even before I knew him, Mumford was my best teacher and guide to New York. The book that formed much of my sense of historic New York was *The Brown Decades,* on the arts in America just after the Civil War, when the brownstones still dominated the residential look of New York. Edith Wharton had of course remembered the brownstones as "cursed with

its universal chocolate-covered coating of the most hideous stone ever quarried." Mumford seized on the brownstone as the drab but authentic symbol of an age utilitarian in everything that nevertheless created lasting, even dominant American forms thanks to the painter Thomas Eakins, the engineers John and Washington Roebling, the architects Henry Hobson Richardson, Louis Sullivan, Daniel Burnham, John Root. He had place for the visionary painter Albert Pinkham Ryder, and could show where Emily Dickinson fitted into the period by reason of her very isolation in Amherst.

Mumford's gift for bringing artistic and technical interests together brought home to me the relationship of the most creative Americans a century ago to the industrial and technological pressures that had become their daily environment. He showed that art and literature came to new life in the age of the factory, the industrial slum, the big city. The most original forms now sprang out of an industrial civilization, in direct relationship to the man-made world. Brooklyn Bridge, Louis Sullivan's Auditorium Building in Chicago, Joseph Morrill Wells's design for McKim, Mead & White at 900 Broadway, Thomas Eakins's supreme rendering of character—all these sprang out of the new age, not in romantic opposition to it. Yet—this was Mumford's special touch—the age itself did not welcome what it made possible. Mumford was fascinated by the industrial-urban scene as an adaptation of human ingenuity to ever-more-proliferating human needs. In his great chapter on the Brooklyn Bridge he showed how engineer Roebling grasped the opportunity for a structure that would command the urban world it served. The materials Roebling worked in, steel and stone, came to work against each other in the final harmony realized by what, after all, was a great machine. Mumford, fascinated by materials, would never be satisfied by technical triumphs alone. He was always pressing for a better life, above all a more deeply satisfying *social* life within the neighborhood as an index to the greater city itself as man's final home.

When *The Brown Decades* came out in 1931, I was sixteen and just finishing high school. I found in Mumford's balancing of so many interests encouragement of my own mental life. There was a disconcerting lot of it for a son of the working class. Unlike my parents, I could never do anything "practical" with my hands. Although I was left alone to read and write, it was my mother, who could neither read nor write, who showed me how to secure the strings in the pegs of my violin, just as, when the time came for my first typewriter, she showed that it was possible to insert a new ribbon without spending half the day at it muddying one's hands.

My inner life was all words, museums, music, libraries. Without knowing that I was preparing myself for the writer's trade, I filled school notebooks I took back from my daily experience of the city. I tutored the spoiled, indolent, fatty sons of dentists in the Bronx. I was a ghostwriter in constant demand by the only wealthy student in my class at City College, a raffish fellow who thought it amusing to have me at his beck and call to write his term papers.

At one point I earned my keep by reading to a blind classmate. He had become a nuisance to his family and had been left to the mercies of the city. I was paid to read aloud William Godwin's *Inquiry Concerning Political Justice* (1793). Godwin, the husband of Mary Wollstonecraft and the father-in-law of Shelley,

was tough but interesting. His style was formal, his thinking so close-knit that the blind student would impatiently stop me, ordering me to reread some difficult passage and discuss its implications.

David Finn also went to City College, graduating in 1943—eight years after I did. With a full program at City he worked full-time as a salesman at the Doubleday Bookshop in Grand Central Station at night, six days a week, from 5:00 P.M. to 12:00 P.M. at a salary of twenty-eight dollars a week, which he gave his parents. He majored in English and, taking "Teddy" Goodman's famous fiction-writing course, was encouraged to think of himself as a future novelist. Goodman was always discovering talent— he had just discovered Jerome Weidman. He told David that while he would probably never equal Joyce, he might, with application, become as good as Aldous Huxley. In my day I had also enrolled in Goodman's course, along with Bernard Malamud. Goodman was not particularly stirred by either of us since we both received a B. I was to enjoy the irony more than Malamud did.

Before I knew it I was a full-fledged literary freelance, getting ten or fifteen dollars a manuscript reading for literary agencies, dramatizing the most frightening stories of Poe for radio performance by actor friends, reviewing for Malcolm Cowley at *The New Republic,* projecting an "as told to" memoir of his spectacular military career in India by a former British colonel holed up at the Gotham Hotel off Fifth Avenue who wanted me to manufacture a best-seller to compete with Francis Yeats-Brown's *Lives of a Bengal Lancer.* After hours of tolerating his condescending manner I would go off to teach evening classes at the New School and City College.

David wanted to be a writer (like his father) but was already painting when he was in the sixth grade. He has been a painter all his life, has had several one-man shows in New York, and has done books of paintings inspired by Yeats's Byzantium poems, Eliot's *Four Quartets* and Keats's *Endymion*. Beginning in 1960, his work as a photographer of sculpture began to overshadow his work as a painter. Growing up on the Upper West Side of Manhattan, he had become another indefatigable walker in the city, haunting Riverside Park and Central Park. "I think I knew every hill and rock and tree in both. I used to walk there alone, often with a sketch pad, doing pencil drawings or watercolors of my favorite spots. I even used to do sketches of people walking on Broadway, the main thoroughfare of my life. I invented a device to enable me to do watercolor sketches in the subway on my way to high school—a medicine dropper filled with brown paint, attached to a paintbrush."

David's paramount visual sense was to make him a pioneer in fields related to the arts. He felt himself fortunate to get a job as a salesman for the American Artists Group, a company founded by Sam Golden on the idea of publishing Christmas cards with reproductions of paintings by well-known contemporary artists, with royalties going to the artists. Accompanied by his wife—they had never been able to get away for their honeymoon—David went around the country with sample bags to show department and stationery stores. He was so successful that he was asked to take over the California territory, but staying in New York, he started (with Bill Ruder) the company called Art in Industry, which used works of art as the basis for design in wallpaper, textiles and the like and then went on to promote such products in a way that built new bridges between the art and business worlds.

Although Art in Industry did not in fact prove to be practical, David and Bill created a monumental presentation book that so impressively explained the idea that they were hired to do promotion and public relations in other fields. Their first clients were musicians, entertainers, a television company, and their first office was a small space that had been a linen closet in the Lombardy Hotel. In the years following, their company grew and grew until it became one of the largest independent public relations companies in the United States. They flourished in the postwar era when many new products were coming on the market, then went on to advise many governments in tourist promotion and economic development, leading colleges and universities, art museums and performing arts groups, companies large and small. Their proudest assignment was at President Kennedy's behest, to gain public support for the Nuclear Test Ban Treaty. Kennedy hoped to create such a ground swell of support for the treaty that it could lead to a whole series of arms control treaties in the years ahead. Otherwise, David says, "We try to stay away from politicians; I have a personal problem with the way public relations tends to be used in politics."

New York in the thirties, our never-to-be-forgotten seedtime, was depressed as well as exciting and raucous. The Federal Writers Project nationally included Ralph Ellison, Saul Bellow, Richard Wright, John Cheever, Conrad Aiken, Harold Rosenberg, Samuel Putnam, Studs Terkel, Katherine Dunham, Frank Yerby, Loren Eiseley, Margaret Walker. There are other well-known names who asked the historian of the writers' project, Jerre Mangione, not to disclose that they had been on the project.

As late as 1941, just before Pearl Harbor, America's median income was $1,070; as many people had annual earnings below that figure as had incomes above it. A migratory farm family earned $1.50 for chopping cotton over a fourteen-hour day. Prices were often lower than they had been in the nineteenth century. It was not unusual to eat a whole dinner for fifty cents in a good restaurant. Relief in New York in one year alone, 1936, public and private, amounted to $310 milllion. A quarter of the work force was unemployed. When FDR came into office in March 1933, the national income was less than $50 billion. On the East River docks a vast emergency shelter housed thousands of men every night. In mid-Manhattan the public squares and parks were filled with homeless men carrying their belongings in paper bags. At the low point of the "crisis" (ended only by the war) one out of three families in New York was in distress. On May Day 1931, when 60,000 people gathered in Union Square to protest unemployment, the police trained machine guns on them.

The fiery Fiorello La Guardia was mayor of New York. By 1938, things had improved just enough for me to get married at twenty-three. New York then was not quite the "world capital" it would become during the war, when some of the greatest European painters thronged Fifty-seventh Street. But even in the thirties New York was the most cosmopolitan of American cities, the center of printing and publishing, one of the country's top manufacturing centers, a major subject of American writing. It was linked to European politics, art, music, literature, by its masses of foreign-born

and their many awake and creative children. Ever since the early twentieth century, (when the *New York Times* became a modern newspaper and a unique resource to educated people), the city typified a restless intelligence in relation to the international scene still unknown in Washington, which until the war was engulfed in the search for national "recovery."

New York in 1938 still saw the El darkening Third, Sixth and Ninth Avenues. Trolleys were still running down Broadway. Little helmeted Greek Mercury figures sat atop the traffic lights on Fifth Avenue. The famous avenue still had double-decker buses (fare: one slim dime) and some of the upper decks were open ones. A *New Yorker* cartoon of the period portraying couples entwined on the upper deck emphasized one couple not entwined. Conductors used to go around with a little machine into which you inserted your dime, and which then rang with a merry clang. The conductor in the cartoon is saying to the one gent on the upper deck not embracing a girl, "Will you please put your arms around her! You're being conspicuous!"

In 1938 all men "going out into business" (and many just going out into the street) wore fedoras and women usually wore hats. Clothes in winter were somber. In Berenice Abbott's lasting photographs of depression crowds crossing Fifth Avenue and Forty-Second Street—for me *the* "crossroads of the world"—you can see how much more formal, mannered, upright and "correct" people were required to look. Broadway was the "Great White Way"; the Palace was the most famous vaudeville house in America. The Paramount, the Astor, the Capitol were "movie palaces" on the same side of Broadway as the Astor Hotel, where Toscanini dwelt when in New York and chased divas down the hall. The RKO Albee in Brooklyn

seemed to be constructed of nothing but marble. Of the New York Paramount it was said, "Its owners spent a million dollars and made every nickel show."

Despite the depression, young people had money and time enough for entertainment. As a young freelance trudging to the *Times* on Forty-third Street in the hope of getting a book to review, I would have to push my way through tremendous crowds outside the Paramount waiting impatiently to hear Frank Sinatra or Benny Goodman. Considering the sleaziness of Eighth Avenue now, it is necessary to remember it fifty years ago as an avenue not only of pawnshops but also of rooming houses and small hotels typifying backstage poverty. The Civic Repertory Theater on Fourteenth Street, where at sixteen I first saw Ibsen, was failing even under the inspired leadership of Eva Le Gallienne. But the Group Theater was at the Belasco and made possible the career of Clifford Odets *(Awake and Sing, Paradise Lost, Golden Boy, Rocket to the Moon).*

How we loved Odets! But also Betty Boop, gravel-voiced Lionel Stander with Noel Coward in Ben Hecht's *Scoundrel* (based on the raffish publisher Horace Liveright), mock-pugnacious Jimmy Durante ("Schnozzola"), the Trans-Lux Newsreel Theater on Broadway where my friend historian Richard Hofstadter and I one day in 1940, looking at lines of tanks and heavy guns lumbering busily, cheerfully out of the factories like new automobiles, solemnly shook hands. The depression was over, and war, blessed war, had come to change our lives forever.

A CREATIVE TOWN

*T*he ultimate modern artist might be defined as someone who likes living in New York City.

—*New York Panorama*
(Federal Writers Project, 1938)

At 32–37 Vernon Boulevard near Thirty-third Street in Long Island City, right along the East River, Manhattan rises up just across the water, positively glares at you as if concentrated in a telescopic lens. Near yet far, pinnacle of self-importance, the legendary towers rise and fall in waves.

This uncelebrated side of the river is industrial and grimy, factories and warehouses, truck depots, sheds, garages, power plants, empty overgrown lots. Everything along these streets speaks of hard, punishing work, heavy things to be made, bulked, hoisted, glazed, sharpened, moved right out. Vernon Boulevard looks as if all the heaviness of New York had descended here and has no desire to look like anything but what it is. So naturally the outdoor sculptors, those muscle men of art, feel right at home here. Mark DiSuvero opened the Socrates Sculpture Park here; there is another called Art on the Beach. The long stretch of urban riverbank extending from the edge of Brooklyn Heights northeast to Long Island City embraces a largely hidden network of avant-garde institutions, outdoor sculptures, historic buildings, fashionable waterfront restaurants. Someone says about Vernon Boulevard, "Art has changed the community. There isn't a sense of menace anymore." Another observer: "Tubes, cement, tiles and brick that seems to have been gathered from demolition sites are shaped into a large insect that seems intent on wrecking everything in sight. Destruction merges with comedy, confusion with order. Brick does not seem like brick, nor pipes like pipes, and everything is turned on its head."

Just along this unbeautiful bank of the river, where Isamu Noguchi first came because there was enough space and heavy machinery for a sculptor whose favorite medium was stone, who worked with the heaviest materials and thought big, is the Noguchi Garden Museum. What was once a photoengraving plant, a long, low, brown brick building, now contains a dazzling sculpture garden. The vast old factory is filled, room on room, with the work of over half a century in stone, basalt, metal, marble, granite, plus Noguchi's designs for playgrounds with playthings (Robert Moses vetoed one such), town plazas, Martha Graham's and Merce Cunningham's dance groups, furniture and Japanese paper lanterns, Sir John Gielgud's production of *King Lear* and the lozenge-shaped swimming pool for Josef von Sternberg. Some of these were never realized.

The sense of artistic self-discovery is everywhere here in the traces of a subtle, delicate and unyielding mind fascinated by the forays it can make into the harshest and heaviest material. Even the variety of trees in the sculpture garden —the great ailanthus, the cherry, the Japanese black pine, the bamboo—testify to Noguchi's labors as something at once totally dedicated yet made playful and witty through his submission to the elemental nature of the material he worked in. In his sunken Japanese garden for the Chase Manhattan Bank Plaza (1960) in the Wall Street area, he featured rocks dug from the bed of the Uji River near Kyoto, each weighing one to five tons and hoisted into position under Noguchi's supervision.

Stone was Noguchi's passion, stone that he revered as the skeletal structure of the earth, stone as the familiar body of every other planet in the solar system with which man has made contact. Stone is the silently enduring figures that surround the quickly disappearing figures of man. With Noguchi, "reverence for the earth" was not a fleeting piety but something actively displayed, visibly reproduced, in hundreds of designs wrought out of stone (but also marble and basalt), each of which has been turned from its inherent monumentality into a startling design. Here they all interlock to reproduce the living symmetry of the great earth itself.

Noguchi liked to get down to the "skin" of the stone he worked in, liked to reveal through his splinterings, hammerings and scrapings the "life" in the stone. When David Finn asked him to pose in the sculpture garden, Noguchi went down on his knees before the low-lying ring of broken stone he had first broken then put together. The breaks are fundamental to his design. He kept touching and retouching his work, constantly glancing back at it as he showed us through his museum, looked as if he could not bear to be parted from what had long been for him the very nature and embodiment of life itself.

What a joy it must have been in one's eighties, and this in Long Island City, to feel that one was working in what Noguchi earnestly called the "essences" and "origins" of life. (He died late in 1988.) The gaping visitor, at first confronting all this rock as intractable and distinctly nonhuman, looking positively lunar, an unrecognizable world like Stonehenge and Easter Island, soon discovered exactly the reverse. Rock here, under Noguchi's hand and eye, affords a passage to everything intrinsic, inherent, subtly interwoven of life itself. The pattern Noguchi liked to resolve was usually austere, veering to the abstract, roughly sloped, even manneristic at times. But with astonishing consistency, he turned each work into a residue of life that we can connect with. We are brought back to the fundamental of our own life in nature: we are all related.

Noguchi said of stone:

It is freedom itself. I love my freedom, and I don't like the restrictions imposed by any mechanical process whether it's with diamond saw, or steel, or whatever. I'm merely involved with the transformation of nature. And nature is infinitely transformable. It comes to life under any circumstance. When you start with stone, and trust and respect the stone, you're always within reach of the origin.

As long as you stay with the earth, you're as free as any creature. Partly indestructible, if you want to call all nature indestructible. What's left is still stone—there's no such thing as an end to a stone.

O nly in New York," finally realizing and bringing to exhibition in an abandoned photoengraving plant, could the diverse influences on the life of this extraordinary man, born in Los Angeles in 1904 of an American mother and Japanese father, have come to such fruition. Had Noguchi still been in California during the roundup and imprisonment of the Nisei, he might have been damaged for life. As it happens, he voluntarily spent months in a Japanese-American relocation camp, Poston Arizona, in order to create landscape environments that were unrealized. He managed to get out of the camp on a "temporary" pass and never bothered to go back.

Noguchi as an artist in New York was a world figure, a distillation of the kind of influences and patterns that make up the very bloodstream of creative New York. Gordon Parks is another. Noguchi in New York was no more startling a presence than was Tom Paine in Greenwich Village, Mozart's librettist Lorenzo da Ponte as a teacher at Columbia and Federico García Lorca as a student there, John Butler Yeats in Chelsea, Leon Trotsky in the Bronx

Isamu Noguchi

and Maxim Gorky on Staten Island, Isaac Bashevis Singer on West Eighty-sixth Street. Thanks to Mussolini, Hitler and Stalin, New York had the pleasure and privilege of receiving Marc Chagall, Ossip Zadkine, Yves Tanguy, Max Ernst, Fernand Léger, André Breton, Piet Mondrian, André Masson, Jacques Lipchitz, Pavel Tchelitchew. Earlier and later it received Béla Bartók, Marcel Duchamp, Hans Hofmann, Arshile Gorky, Willem de Kooning, Saul Steinberg. Not to forget, under other circumstances, W. H. Auden, Henri Cartier-Bresson, Ilya Bolotowsky and Gabriel García Marquez, who said after his experiences on the staff of a Spanish-language paper that he had a "tropical" memory of New York. "It was like no place else. It was putrefying, but it was also in the process of rebirth, like the jungle. It fascinated me."

On Yom Kippur 1943, the Jewish Day of Atonement, Marc Chagall, encountered at Madison and Fifty-seventh Street, and cheerfully talking Yiddish—"I haven't heard so much of the mother tongue since I left Vitebsk!" —confessed that New York had also given him the tremors about working on the holy day. "So I thought I would drop in on Pierre Matisse's gallery." Delmore Schwartz was right, at least during the war. "Europe is still the biggest thing in North America."

There was an unmistakable flow of new life, the sense of creative new direction, an authoritatively bold sense of style. This was to have the most tremendous effect on the social realists and WPA muralists of the 1930s who were soon won to abstract expressionism as a more genuinely native style. The fate of the first abstract murals in the United States, painted in the 1930s by four of the founders of American abstract artists, shows how difficult it was until the war for painters who rejected social realism. Led by Ilya Bolotowsky, the best-known artist of the group, they did abstract murals for the Williamsburgh Housing Project in Brooklyn. These were recently recovered in basement storage areas and offices covered by as many as eight coats of wall paint, in two instances painted with rubber cement so they could be used as self-adhesive bulletin boards.

The overwhelming prosperity that came with the war, the glitter that came after the war and has never left, seemed to deride the all-too-purposeful social realism of the thirties. In 1944 the government sold out of its warehouses, at four cents a pound, the work of the many artists it had supported during the depression. The most prominent abstract expressionists—Rothko, Adolph Gottlieb, Barnett Newman—were radicals of the thirties who in their own minds remained radical in the face of wartime horrors. Just as the large WPA frescoes remained an influence on Rothko's visionary new style, so he said that he started "with arbitrary forms or shapes and tried to come from that to something that relates to life and evokes and expresses some of the feelings we are concerned with today, such as the disintegration of the world." As Robert Motherwell said of the postwar scene, a premonition of disaster was a very natural feeling for someone in the forties to be dealing with.

A French critic in America, Serge Guilbaut, wrote that New York "stole the idea of modern art," and ascribed abstract expressionism to a wartime prosperity, a new sense of luxury and excess, that beginning with the art boom in 1944 made high culture part of the consumer economy. The irresistible opulence made for a

"rearrangement of the social hierarchy." Guilbaut found political menace in all this, a reshaping of American interests that drove even intellectuals and artists to accept the Cold War.

What was missing in this indictment was the unmistakable effect on American artists of the verve and imagination that some extraordinary Europeans in New York had saved from war's devastation. If New York was finally at home with high modernism, on its way to replacing Paris as the center of Western art, there were good historic reasons. A main reason was New York. There is something about New York that is eternally congenial to exiles. Those who have been aloft too long soon sense that here they can *land*. For painters, sculptors, designers of every sort who need no further language, New York is a theater of the will that quickly reveals many opportunities. New York today as the great marketplace and showplace of art, positively the greatest manufactory of art—whether real, pretended, or just intended—lent itself to exiles who had no fear of having to sacrifice any native tradition *here*.

It was all the bustle and Rialto of Art, Art, Art in the East Village, Soho, Tribeca, Queens, elusive settlements in Brooklyn and off Newtown Creek, more thousands of people making Art than had been seen since New York ceased to be the country's fifth largest manufacturing center. Artists feel at home here. Says the English-born *New York Times* art critic John Russell,

ours is the city where a great many English painters and sculptors most want to be. . . . All things are possible there. Art matters, in ways not often met with in London. The level of energy is unimaginably high. Ideas abound. Inspiration comes with the morning milk. Talk is free and frank. Human relationships burgeon with startling rapidity. Not only do laymen like to look at art and talk about it, but they like to buy it and take it home. How should the English exile not be happy?

London in the early 1960s might have seemed expansive. "But there was something about the openness and spontaneity of human exchange in New York that came as a revelation." Russell might have added, as the English usually do, "There is something about New York that causes people to need less sleep here." They certainly get less.

What new arrivals did not know was that New York had never looked so bright and frisky before. The El had long made great avenues like Third, Sixth and Ninth dark, "picturesque" and cuddlesome. Suddenly they were thrown open to the light. While this made for a lost joy in New York—looking into other people's windows—the astonishing look of "new" Third Avenue and the gleaming new structures of glass everywhere made one remember Frank Lloyd Wright's dream for New York back in 1928. Wright imagined a city "iridescent by day, luminous by night, imperishable! Buildings, shimmering fabrics, woven of rich glass; glass all clear or part opaque and part clear, patterned in color or stamped to harmonize with the metal tracery that is to hold all together."

The open light was a constant stimulus. It was impossible to look at a pioneer, lovably old-fashioned New York realist of the ashcan school like John Sloan without recognizing how much painters had depended for "atmosphere" on the darkness made by the El. In Sloan it was the startling red or green on the wide, sweeping hat of a secretary, glimpsed under the black iron lines of the "elevated railroad," that gave such vivacity to the painting as was not obtained from street lamps.

New York painting once meant painting New York itself, was intensely local. Every touch of Sloan's New York, especially before the "Great War," is tender, domestic. His back alleys, shop and factory girls under the Sixth Avenue El at the rush hour give the impression that he wants to portray New York in some loving atmosphere of discovery. New York had not yet been locked into mass society. People moved in friendly groups and associations, not as the lonesome crowd. Women fervently dressed up, their one chance to shine, provide in their opulent figures the zip as well as the color missing from the roofs where people are sleeping of a hot summer night, the hooded figures on the line of unemployed men waiting in the snow at Fifth and Madison Square for the hot coffee that was being offered by one of the newspapers.

The neighborliness—above all the leisureliness—constantly portrayed in Sloan's old New York, the easy views of what is going on behind so many unshaded night windows—all now an astonishment as a subject for art. The essential thing now about painting New York is to do the city as a theory. New York even for native-born artists is not a homeland but a situation. It is a problem to be solved in competition with other artists. The deracinating influence of modernism is unmistakable, as is the fierceness, breathlessness, recklessness brought to the struggle for recognition. If no artist is more home here than anyone else, the battleground of contemporary styles is home enough. What counts is to astonish, and the foreign-born eye can be a decisive influence, or a master of the revels, just by showing that the city requires not love but freedom and ingenuity.

A young English painter in New York, Rackstraw Downes, has a canvas titled *IRT Elevated Station at Broadway and 125th*. The grubby station in the valley below the upper tracks is just a

detail. The picture is a wide-screen panorama, tilted to one side, dizzying but intensely realistic in its detail. You are as totally outside the picture as if you were crossing it by plane, yet helplessly drawn back into astonishing replicas of what you have known on foot, day by day in your own life. The distortion is impressive but fatiguing, highly theoretical in twentieth-century fashion, in the end just another "idea." There is no sense of place, not even of New York being mimicked—just some helpless sense of intimidation before what Downes has caught so brilliantly, the sheer weight, the imponderability of so many unlovely structures. "What can I *do* with this?" one seems to hear him saying. "How can I get the better of it?"

American artists-to-be once went to Europe to learn tradition, classicism, models for life. Europeans come to New York to observe more closely a civilization so utilitarian that it engages all their frolic power. I have never forgotten the Swiss sculptor Jean Tinguely's *Homage to New York,* which was performed rather than shown at the Museum of Modern Art, failed to destroy itself as programmed and caused a fire. Of course this too could have been called *Study for an End of the World.* New York as some kind of apex of mechanical civilization inspires such thoughts. Tinguely's was a huge construction "whose sole purpose was to destroy itself in one glorious act of mechanical suicide." The piece was composed of scrap metal, bicycle parts, a washing machine drum, an upright piano, a radio, several electric fans, an old Addressograph, a baby's bassinet, three dozen bicycle and baby carriage wheels, uncounted small motors and fan belts, two motor-driven devices that produce instant abstract paintings by the yard, several bottles of chemical stinks, an apparatus to make smoke, bells and klaxons and other

Saul Steinberg

noisemakers, and yards and yards of metal tubing. The entire apparatus was painted white and topped by an inflated orange meteorological balloon.

Of all exiled and displaced artists who settled into New York during the war as if to awaken the material city to its hidden self, none has been so successful, even sovereign, in imposing his imagination upon the city as Saul Steinberg. Steinberg in New York, Steinberg in his covers and cartoons for *The New Yorker,* Steinberg at the Betty Parsons Gallery, the Sidney Janis and how many others since he first startled the art mob at the Wakefield in 1943. Steinberg at galleries and special exhibitions in Washington, Paris, Milan, Cologne, Amsterdam, Stockholm. Steinberg in the many book collections of his drawings has long been an instantly recognizable original, a signature, calligraphy and trademark for fantasies, ruminations and satires woven like Ariadne's thread straight from the pen that never seems to leave his hand.

The very name "Steinberg" and his oeuvre became each other's trademark. This was his inability to deviate from a special course that *seemed* to consist in turning calligraphy and a child's "primitive" style of drawing into endless variations of the human figure and the (once unbelievable) alternatives to "reality" locked up in the human head. "I am among the few," he says in his matter-of-fact style, "who continue to draw after childhood is ended, continuing and perfecting childhood drawing without the traditional interruption of childhood training," And: "I loved to arrive in a new place and face the new situations like one newly born for the first time, when it still has the air of fiction.

(This lasts one day.)" One sees in his revolving show of New York streets and faces the ferocity of overwhelming buildings and crowds suffered by the newcomer. Steinberg the pilgrim in the New World—always a new one—draws his progress through a world so much heavier than himself that he has to lighten, reduce and fantasize it.

The *faux-naif* style of children's drawing was easily accepted because of its impish lucidity and has been much copied. But what counts most with Steinberg is the truly gifted man's inability to respect prevailing opinion. The conventional world confronts Steinberg as material to be turned by *him*. One of the wittiest artists of the century, he is in person—see David Finn's photograph—essentially severe, magisterial, kindly but by no means humble. Permitting himself to be photographed, Steinberg immediately put on a settled, determined look, fixed on whatever in space he wanted at that moment to think about. A look characterized by tightly drawn lips expressive of determination, independence and polite surprise at what strange people he is forever meeting with; although he is just looking into space, courteously lending himself to the occasion, the fixity of the face under the dominating spectacles makes the deepest impression. A sort of professional visitor, he is very conscious of being himself and no other, yields nothing in the way of sentiment or easy obligingness. Steinberg is always Steinberg.

He is not just an image maker, a professional artist as the type goes. He thinks and thinks, is so reflective and even judgmental that that his conversation is heavy, seems an extension of the intricately woven labyrinth that is his work. Perhaps he feels a need to reconstitute the world as it is, to replace it with Steinbergs. No wonder that he admires certain novelists more than graphic artists. The supposedly "real" world was long ago made unreal by what he caustically remembers as Turkish primitivism and decadence, the Balkan rottenness of the Rumania he grew up in. But his father made boxes, as in a sense *he* does still. Wherever he lives, everything is laid out as neatly and severely as the lines of a Steinberg drawing.

Then there was the absurdity of studying architecture in Milan, arduous training in the classical style Steinberg loves antically to build on and use up. This when Il Duce took up Der Führer's campaign against Jews. Steinberg's diploma as *Dottore in Architettura,* bestowed on Saul Steinberg of the "Israelite race" in the name of the Kingdom of Italy and His Majesty Vittorio Emmanuele, gives Steinberg invincible pleasure. Nothing and nobody on that precious document—not the Kingdom of Italy or His Majesty Vittorio Emmanuele II— has survived except Saul Steinberg of the "Israelite race."

Steinberg's work appeared in America before he did—in *Life* and *Harpers Bazaar.* He left Italy via Lisbon for Santo Domingo. Only in July 1942 was he able to enter the United States as an immigrant, landing in Miami and continuing by bus to New York. Whereupon, the inimitable Steinberg touch, he was commissioned an ensign in the United States Navy and was sent out to the Far East, attached to the Fourteenth Air Force. Saul Steinberg, U.S. Navy, with very little English, was of official use in communicating with our Asian allies by means of his drawings. The displaced Steinberg has never gotten over the importance of papers, diplomas, passports, visas. They recur in his work with sinister importance. The exile's precious document, full of pompously

illegible handwriting, signed with the usual European bureaucratic signature in exaggerated flourishes, is a central image for Steinberg. It is a necessity, a trap, a hindrance, but the only way out of Europe.

In New York the much-traveled artist found a special home in *The New Yorker.* What has always distinguished this magazine is the sense of style that came with its origins in the 1920s, a sense of the immediately right effect that a word must produce. Steinberg at first might have seemed outré; there were complaints from long-settled minds on the staff that he was "cruel." His satire was perhaps too universal to make the immediate effect journalism requires.

But in a magazine so brilliantly practiced in graphic values, Steinberg's originality spoke for itself. It was a moment when "Art New York" became the symbol in "action painting" of autonomous self-expression, recklessness and provocation, of pop art as both a determined parody of the insatiable consumer culture and as homage to it. Originality real or merely willful was everyday currency.

"Steinberg" became a signature, a trademark, constant evidence of how much taste had been extended in every direction. Incorporating Steinberg's almost weekly drawings, *The New Yorker* elevated itself from the self-reflexive chic of its founding spirits. But Steinberg was a puzzle to many, still placeable as a "cartoonist" even though his whimsy mounted into the purest hair-raising fantasy. *The New Yorker* and its staff became a part of Steinberg's own imagination. In conversation he ruminated that the magazine's long-time editor, William Shawn (obsessed with the magazine before he joined the staff), now made "a sort of novel" of his own as he put together the week's different contents.

Life in America certainly bore a different face after 1945. Down in Mississippi, poorest state in the Union, William Faulkner said, "They've just licked the Krauts and Japs and are going to crush the world with money." Mississippi didn't know the half of it. In New York it seemed to many interesting minds that with Europe gone, the political order gone, all moral order in question, the whole life experience was subjective, open to grabs, a game, a gamble, a test of one's metaphysical daring in the face of so much public emptiness. Steinberg in his antic constructions became a favorite text of so much displacement. In his art the once official, material, external, judgmental world was dematerialized. All mundane wearisomely routine things lost "body" under Steinberg's unstoppable pen. The world was suddenly weightless, the human brain hollow except for its fantasies—which performed their own lives at the pleasure of the pen.

The sign replaced the word. This was not unpleasing to a new class of sophisticated professionals, an elite born of the ever-dominating technology, a group far more numerous and adept at social definition than the old intelligentsia founded on the word, and thus always guilty and nostalgic at the abandonment of its utopianism. Steinberg's popularity, like the sheer power-in-volume of abstract expressionism, was further proof that with the ascendancy of the sign over the word there was no longer any clear direction into a future. The graphic arts flourish in association with wealth, sweeping building programs, bold new innovations in architecture. As New York seemed to recreate itself after the war, the great symbol of its infatuation with itself was the visual as it made its triumphant progress from the show windows of the great shops and department stores through the magazines to the art galleries and museums where Art became the most desired form of capital.

An immediate effect of this: literary intellectuals and unattached voyeurs saw that art was the only serious game in town and required their analytic talents far more than literature did. New York had always been critic country. No other city had the magazines, the tradition of the independent commentator and guardian of the arts when literature was still the queen of the arts. Edgar Allan Poe, Henry James, William Dean Howells, John Jay Chapman to Henry Mencken, Van Wyck Brooks, Randolph Bourne, Edmund Wilson, Malcolm Cowley, Lionel Trilling. The "metropolitan critic," as Edmund Wilson was almost the last to typify the role, was the critic who drew his curiosity, force and widespread interests from the many-charged life of the city.

This depended on an insurgent tradition, the need to connect literature with society and to show through literature what was neglected, suppressed and dangerous in society itself. The poet Randall Jarrell laughed that certain critics after the war—he was probably thinking of Lionel Trilling—had the power over certain couples once possessed by a liberal clergyman. In the days to come, the influence of art and film critics reminded one of peasant mothers who chewed up their babies' food for them. These critics told you just how to look at a picture, a movie. Their influence was sort of total; there was no mistaking what you were meant to see and how to think about it forever after.

The insurgent tradition did not appeal to the throngs of "pure critics" now welcome in the universities. The most joyous task of criticism, to seek out the really "new" and to get recognition for it, fell to literary intellectuals-turned-art critics—Clement Greenberg and Harold Rosenberg were among the most notable examples. They were vehemently independent radicals, long seasoned in defiant postures by the (now defunct) radical movement and the magazine *Partisan Review,* which had united radicalism and modernism as a single cause. Greenberg was to become *the* guru of the day for many painters and sculptors; he helped to change and direct styles as his friends and admirers came to think like him. Rosenberg, more purely speculative, always the intellectual in the old polemical tradition, never gave the impression of leading the artists he was always writing about. They were food for thought, *his* thought. With his terrific instinct for trends, he gave the impression that literature (except for criticism like his own) was out, painting as the newest form of "action" was in.

Rosenberg raised to the "tradition of the new" the special company of the New York school—Mark Rothko, Barnett Newman, Adolph Gottlieb, Arshile Gorky, David Smith, Willem de Kooning, Philip Guston, Hans Hofmann, Franz Kline, Robert Motherwell, Jackson Pollock, Ad Reinhardt, Clyfford Still, Bradley Walker Tomlin. Although these did not all live near Rosenberg in the Springs section of the Hamptons in eastern Long Island, he somehow turned this ultrafashionable rural scene into a suburb of New York devoted entirely to art. And art was devoted to New York's twentieth-century tradition of insurgent intellect. Happy Days were here again, New York was back to itself. From the first exhibitions of the New York school at the Museum of Modern Art and the Metropolitan Museum of Art, it was made known that "it is against the background of New York artists that all current American art must be viewed. Virtually every important American artist to have emerged in the last fifteen years looks to the achievement of American abstract expressionism as a point of departure, in the same way that most European artists of the 1920s and 1930s referred in their work to the inventions of cubism."

There's nothing like a *movement* to rouse the energies, to give a sense of purpose, to be stimulated by friendly controversy with one's crowd. Literary modernism represented by Joyce, Eliot and Pound was now safely interred in the English departments, where it was not wise to go outside the canon. But in *New York,* now the "world capital of art and the successor to Paris," painting was modernism, was once again revolution, defiance, irresistible as it astonished in every line. Harold Rosenberg's unsuppressed Marxist interests called it "action art," noted that the untrammeled artist was now free to "fuck up the canvas." Painters anyway have more zip than writers, and at any convivial gathering of painters out in the Hamptons, amidst the laughter, the uproar and the dizzying sense of unexpected wealth pouring in on this crowd in work clothes, one had again the sense, yes, that there had been no such excitement since October 1917. People were alive and vehement to the most astonishing degree. The world was new again.

When David Riesman and William Whyte worried about "the lonely crowd," the "organization man," the bureaucratization of American intellect, Rosenberg replied, "The critics of the new America are disheartened by a revolution won—their revolution, which can go no further than the ending of the underground life of the American intellectual mass through economic recognition of the services it has to offer. With his own success achieved, the only issue the intellectual can see as remaining for society is 'personality.' And the result, as Whyte says, is that since the war no novel or play has given body to the larger disturbances of the American consciousness.''

Were the writers really this out of it now? In 1948 two bristlingly talented writers almost of an age, Truman Capote and Norman Mailer, both definitely "outsiders" to conventional opinion, became famous the same season with their first novels, *Other Voices, Other Rooms* and *The Naked and the Dead.* Capote's photograph on the jacket received as much comment as the book. Not since the young Cleopatra introduced herself to Caesar by unrolling herself out of a rug had there been such "an advertisement for myself." The androgynously pretty Mr. Capote, big eyes looking up from under blond bangs, and wearing a tattersall vest, reclined sensually on a sofa. Capote had put as much thought into this showpiece as he did into the muted, subtly melancholy story of a precocious teenager's descent into sexual self-knowledge.

"I had to be successful," Capote ruminated in later years over his initial success, "and I had to be successful early. The thing about people like me is that we always knew what we were going to do. Many people spend half their lives not knowing, and I had to have a very special life. I was not meant to work in an office or something, though I would have been successful at whatever I did. But I always knew that I wanted to be a writer and that I wanted to be rich and famous."

The subtly illicit side of this astonishing debut was precocious Capote's androgyny. It made him seem not so much different as cleverer. Until he erred near the end of his life by think-

ing that they would enjoy his cleverness about *them,* the unsettling face and body of the pretty little man had the most rousing effect on the wealthiest. He really lent himself to people; he charmed by sheer vividness. What charmed was not just his sassiness and intuitive sense of other people but his determination to be accepted on his own terms by any company in which he chose to shine.

"You see," he once said, "I was so different from everyone, so much more intelligent and sensitive and perceptive. I was having fifty perceptions a minute to everyone else's five. I always felt that nobody was going to understand me, going to understand what I felt about things. I guess that's why I started writing. At least on paper I could put down what I thought."

To which he added that in person he had always been so irresistible that "everyone had me. Including fire hydrants."

The impishly provocative little southerner was actually as good a writer as he said he was. The public image and the "artist" (Capote insisted on this definition of himself) coalesced. Yet he would never write believable fiction about adult men and women; his characters were marginal types. He was a miniaturist, maker of elegant boxes like the painter-craftsman Joseph Cornell. At the heart of Capote's fiction and reportage (the apex of his work was *In Cold Blood* with its unforgettable contrast of the innocent-conventional Clutters and their killers) was his sense of transiency in all things, of homelessness and some fatal unattachment. One always feels about Capote's characters, real and fictional, that the rooms they live in are essentially bare, that as with Holly Golightly's domestic arrangements in *Breakfast at Tiffany's* the blouse needed for the gala evening out can be found at the last possible moment—under the bed. The Clutters in *In Cold Blood* are rich in family and American possessions—much good it does them! Capote's unmistakable yearning toward the killers is founded on the fact that they and Capote together are birds of passage.

Such dispossession—and ultimate hollowness of heart—could be called the character of the era. Everything, especially in "the capital of the world," was richer, more opulent, more soigné than ever—and mercilessly in transit. This sense of transiency, when combined with so many fashionable airs, made an irresistible combination for Capote. Dispossession carried into modern riches, all shallow things, had long been the southerner's *cri de coeur*. The deepest southern imagination to arise after the war, Flannery O'Connor, could not tolerate New York, described it as death in the air. Capote's appeal and underlying theme, his *frisson,* music, was poignant in its own way, but not brittle or sentimental. The world was full of things, every street in New York could be taken as a party. In *Breakfast at Tiffany's:*

Another night, deep in the summer, the heat of my room sent me out into the street. I walked down Third Avenue to Fifty-first Street, where there was an antique store with an object in its window I admired: a palace of a bird cage, a mosque of minarets and bamboo rooms yearning to be filled with talkative parrots. But the price was three hundred and fifty dollars. On the way home I noticed a cab-driver crowd gathered in front of P. J. Clarke's saloon, apparently attracted there by a happy group of whiskey-eyed Australian army officers baritoning "Waltzing Matilda." As they sang, they took turns spin-dancing a girl over the cobbles under the El; and the girl, Miss Golightly, to be sure, floated round in their arms light as a scarf.

Norman Mailer, who admired Capote as an utterly sound workman, had the same genius for getting to the public. Where Capote suggested a certain air of weary experience, as if it were his fatality, Mailer worked his personal fantasies to the sky, hoarsely upheld sex as ideology. If it sometimes looked as if the postwar novel in America had just discovered sex, emancipated Jewish writers thrived on it. Their underlying subject was the novelty of divorce. Mailer, in this as in everything else, was beyond everyone. His favorite fantasy of himself was the novelist as superstar, replacing Hemingway, displacing everyone in his own war generation. At the same time he dreamed of being a Cause —a whole series of Causes—with himself as standard bearer and the adversary of everything even minutely conventional. His gift for promoting himself was a tribute to his leading such an active dream life in public. "Orgy," group sex, public sex, always a far-out response to every intimacy of life—all became burning issues of life personal and political, mixed with the scandal that came from living everything out in public. Mailer was unique. No other writer seemed so lacking in inhibitions and qualifications. The mind behind this seemed insatiable, forever pumping up the sound of battle from Mailer's internal landscape.

The Naked and the Dead, Mailer's catapult into early fame and the big money, was the last Popular Front novel, full of GI decency and a Fascist-minded colonel. Its narrative devices owed everything to Dos Passos and social novels of the 1930s. The book made Mailer so prominent that he decided he could unlock himself now to a higher destiny.

This was to "work a revolution in our consciousness." Calling himself "the boldest writer

to have come out of my flabby time," hinting that he was almost afraid to face the full magnitude of the American epic he was preparing to write, this was going to be too bold for the publishers,

. . . I do not have the confidence that you will see it in its completed form, except as an outlaw of the underground like *Tropic of Cancer, Ulysses,* or Sade's *Hundred and Twenty Days of Sodom.* . . . The book will be fired to its fuse by the rumor that once I pointed to the farthest fence and said that within ten years I would try to hit the longest ball ever to go up into the accelerted hurricane air of our American letters. For if I have one ambition above all others, it is to write a novel which Dostoevsky and Marx; Joyce and Freud; Stendhal, Tolstoy, Proust and Spengler; Faulkner, and even old moldering Hemingway might come to read, for it would carry what they had to tell another part of the way.

This was not only out of scale with what was going on in American writing, but with Mailer's real gifts for "conspiracy," as in *Barbary Shore* and for satire in *The Deer Park,* brilliant political fiction on the anti-Red hysteria of the period. Of course *The Deer Park* was full of sexual obsessions, just as *An American Dream* was to contain some hair-raising descriptions of New York along with Mailer's usual need to consult his internal prompter, his fantasy life, about the effect of the moon. The frustrated radical in Mailer found strange outlets in the gospel of sex and of violence as "courage." Why was this very talented man always pushing himself to say something *still* more outrageous? The most indelible of his orations was "The White Negro"—the hipster of the 1950s had to be an outlaw, just like the Negro!

It can of course be suggested that it takes little courage for two strong eighteen-year-old hoodlums, let us say, to beat in the brains of a candy-store keeper, and indeed the action even by the logic of the psychopath is not likely to prove very therapeutic, for the victim is not an immediate equal. Still, courage of a sort is necessary, for one murders not only a weak fifty-year-old man but an institution as well, one violates private property, one enters into a new relation with the police and introduces a dangerous element into one's life. The hoodlum is therefore daring the unknown, and so no matter how brutal the act, it is not altogether cowardly.

Mailer was a natural celebrity for a time of endless turmoil—one that now seemed to warrant only psychological responses. He locked his work and persona vehemently together in a fashion that was now a New York standard. He told *Rolling Stone* in 1975: "The ambition of a writer like myself is to become consecutively more disruptive, more dangerous, and more powerful." In those days he and his then disciple Norman Podhoretz went about in black leather jackets as if looking for a fifty-year-old candy-store keeper. By the eighties one never saw Mailer in newspaper photographs without a dinner jacket. Somehow one associates Mailer the natural celebrity always with matters of dress—and undress. At the height of orgy-as-politics Mailer stood his ground at a party absolutely bottomless, walking about with the ease of a seasoned lecturer before a women's club. The sight was in no way remarkable, but imagine the contrast before so many fully clothed people and, in the middle, Norman without even his shorts! His then wife, a Latin-looking beauty and naked, looked sour. Norman looked up to her every few minutes like a pitcher leaving the mound to confer with his catcher. She whispered. He shook his head. Something new was needed. She looked more and more impatient. To my great delight, I heard her say "Shit, Norman! These characters are too timid for us."

There was quite a contrast here with old Isaac Bashevis Singer on West Eighty-sixth Street off Broadway, always in a blue suit, white shirt and tie. He looked formidably European and correct in contrast with the informal Americans who had come to photograph him, but more than a little diffident. The extreme hesitancy on his face said: Do these people know what they are doing?

When Singer arrived in the 1930s (what luck for all of us), he knew where his next meal was coming from only when Abraham Cahan at the *Jewish Daily Forward* indifferently bought a story or a feuilleton. He subsisted in cafeterias and Sea Gate boardinghouses among Yiddish speakers. They may well have been deceived by his familiar accent and submissive, anxiously civil manner. This man out of tormented Poland wants no trouble. He has never ceased to feel himself a stranger here. But that may have as much to do with the obligations of his craft as it does with his wish for a quiet life. Singer is the last nineteenth-century novelist—cast up on the twentieth-century shore in the most turbulent of world cities to depict a traditional way of life in Poland between the wars that was being squeezed out of existence even before Hitler arrived to murder three million Jews.

Having come here before the war, Singer is not exactly a "survivor." But given his uniqueness and all he has to tell, he might well say, as is foretold in the book of Job: "And I only am escaped alone to tell thee."

To Singer, brought up in the strictest orthodoxy (no friend of "profane" literature), has the strange mission been given. To recreate, in the mother tongue of Eastern European Jews, so often patronized as "jargon" and derided, and this in story after story, the life of a whole peo-ple still bound (whether they knew it or not) to the ancient reservoir of belief in which they had their being. But this is putting it externally. What Singer understood was that the tradition of the "fathers" could be too strong for their descendants. They were only human beings, and caught in a social trap, isolated from other Poles, that enabled the Nazis to finish them off. And what was more central to fiction than people too weak and disordered, constantly under fire, to be equal to all the holy obligations they took as their reason for being?

Singer was not like anyone else. He was interested in the Jew as sinner, sensualist, unwitting skeptic, the Jew ground between the millstones of religious duty and the abysses of a deceitful world. He brought some startling interests to storytelling. The arcane side of his religious background gave him a gleeful acquaintance with magic, superstition, the minor deities and devils attending the supernatural concerns of the traditional Jew. And he was fascinated by the challenge that sexuality presented to the self-image of the Jew, by irrepressible instinct in the face of so many taboos. He avoided sentimentalizing Jews because they were usually powerless. Singer was all too aware that oppression does not improve the character.

Singer did not go after fame in America. A writer in Yiddish was hardly in a position to do so, and in any event the reserved and correct Singer was busy writing for a living. He sometimes contributed so much to a single issue of the *Forward* that he needed a pseudonym, "Warshavsky"—from Warsaw. It was still inconceivable to him that a large American—even international—audience would be available to him in translation.

Eventually Singer became so much a part of the national literary scene that he jokingly said he wrote in two languages at once. Singer became a hero to American Jews suddenly awake to the fact that the "old world" was so compelling—and universal. It seemed that on the unfashionable Upper West Side of New York there lived a vegetarian who haunted Jewish dairy restaurants and Greek coffee shops, talked English in an accent one had been taught to despise—and this man was actually and unbelievably a master, and on his way to becoming a world figure.

As David Finn prepared to photograph him, Singer insisted on posing in the center of what —in reply to his wife Alma's horror of it—he calls his "garbage room." This remarkably disordered room holds his identical blue suits— and hung jauntily, every which way on the walls, the tributes Singer has received from every conceivable group, not forgetting the Jewish lawyers of Texas. Honors have been thrust on him in such profusion that Singer, both overwhelmed and amused, has heaped everything together in resignation to his amazing popularity. Over one bookcase, hung as indifferently as the rest, is the Nobel Prize.

I have never lived so close to blacks before. The only significance is that there isn't any. As with everybody else in this busy, busy structure, there is no prolonged conversation, just witty grumblings when the elevators fail or when the landlord's drive to co-op becomes hot and heavy. An anxious civility, a tense watchfulness, as we open and hold doors for each other when the shopping is fierce. As the old Nichols and May line had it, "There is proximity but no relating."

The only blacks I have ever "known" in any sense have been superb writers: Richard Wright, Ralph Ellison, James Baldwin, Gordon Parks.

Wright, the most moving of them and the moodiest—in this he had a lot of competition— was of course very formal in the days when it was still an event for black and white writers to sit down together in a midtown restaurant. Frank's in Harlem was something else. Born in Mississippi, fatherless, brought up in the severest poverty, Wright grew up under conditions resembling peonage. His grandparents had been slaves. He made his way to Chicago, where he worked in the post office. As he wrote in "The Man Who Went to Chicago": "What could I dream of that had the barest possibility of coming true? I could think of nothing. And, slowly, it was upon exactly that nothingness that my mind began to dwell."

His chance to write came through the Federal Writers Project. In 1932, as the depression deepened, he became a Communist and married a Jewish "comrade"; they had a child. Those were the now unbelievable days of black-Jewish togetherness. Whatever hopeful propaganda the Communists may have expected of a black recruit from deepest, darkest Mississippi, poorest state in the Union, Wright quickly revealed in the stories of *Uncle Tom's Children* that he thought of America as a "nothing" situation for the black man. You did not have to read Dick Wright to sense the intimacy with some sense of doom that this handsome, deeply gifted man carried around with him. But in every story but one of *Uncle Tom's Children* the hero's search for a better life ends in death. And in his most powerful and most celebrated book, *Native Son,* which can be a shocker for people unprepared to face the depth of Wright's case against white America, one saw at the same time the implacable logic with which Wright took his blundering, accidental murderer, Bigger Thomas, to the electric chair. There was simply no way out

Isaac Bashevis Singer

for Bigger Thomas. There was apparently no way out for characters doomed just by the nature of their place in situations starkly named *Black Boy, Uncle Tom's Children, Native Son,* "The Man Who Lived Underground," *The Outsider.*

Wright left the Communist party and had bitter things to say, along with white intellectuals like Arthur Koestler, about "the god that failed." He was exasperated by the housing difficulties even a famous black writer experienced in Greenwich Village, left the United States for what he hoped was a more positive situation in Paris under the auspices of Jean-Paul Sartre. Quest after quest for this homeless, easily wounded man from Mississippi. Sartre no doubt did his best for Wright, enlisted him among other "mandarins" in his anti-American campaigns. Of course Sartre thought of Wright as a symbol. And Sartre did not know English. Wright was only fifty-two when he died in Paris in 1960.

Wright, the most haunting black writer of the time, felt a failure, somehow died a failure far from home. My occasional friend Ralph Ellison became with *Invisible Man* black literature's first great national success. It was fascinating to observe his ascent on the American scene. He had been so poor in Oklahoma during the depression that he had gone out shooting birds to feed his family. Tuskegee Institute, of which Ellison made such brilliant satiric use in *Invisible Man,* had been followed by hard knocks as a jazz trumpeter, ship's cook during the war, the usual disillusionment—in Harlem—with Communists. All the while Ralph *Waldo* Ellison, named after Emerson, was struggling to find his own voice as a writer. His problem, as he dramatized it brilliantly in *Invisible Man,* was as age-old as the first black preacher: eloquence

was altogether too near and dear to him. The young man in the novel constantly lends his gift for speech to one corrupter, misleader, exploiter of his people after another. He cannot stop speechifying, "performing," and he cannot stop doing it for people who can use him. It is only when he is chased into a cellar, which is where the book begins, that he finds his own voice. And what a voice:

I can hear you say, "What a horrible, irresponsible bastard." And you're right. I leap to agree with you. I am one of the most irresponsible beings that ever lived. Irresponsibility is part of my invisibility; any way you face it, it is a denial. But to whom can I be responsible, and why should I be, when you refuse to see me? And wait until I reveal how truly irresponsible I am. Responsibility rests upon recognition, and recognition is a form of agreement. Take the man whom I almost killed: Who was responsible for that near murder—I? I don't think so, and I refuse it. I won't buy it. You can't give it to me. *He* bumped *me, he* insulted *me.* Shouldn't he, for his own personal safety, have recognized my hysteria, my "danger potential"?

Invisible Man came out at a time, the early 1950s, when a book of such power, wit and searing truthfulness had a chance to penetrate the hard crust of American racism. It was a work of art, it satisfied as a work of art, it has lasted as a work of art. Ellison was not only honored as no other black writer had been before; he was honestly *welcomed* into a place long waiting for just such a writer in the national community of letters. He was another brilliant southerner by origin who could say how much Faulkner had influenced him even when the word "nigger" appeared on every page.

Ellison was a natural star: and with a voice, the almost-too-beautiful voice he had paraded and satirized in *Invisible Man,* to match. But being, in the ridiculous language of American publicity and salesmanship, a "minority," he had somehow to prove himself. He was the author of an undoubted American "classic," represented Lyndon Johnson abroad, graced the most distinguished academic chairs in America, had even won the United States' highest civilian award, the Medal of Freedom. But the question at the ringside was increasingly: "Where is Ralph's second book? When will he repeat his first triumph?"

Ellison's splendid voice sometimes cracked and grew shrill at public ceremonies. There was a lot of strain and malignant bad luck: much of a new manuscript was lost in a fire. There was a constant silent interrogation of his literary future —it was hard not to see this for white mockery. When Irving Howe urged him to be more radical, Ellison spoke proudly of his art, compared it to the hunting of birds. As black writers became more numerous, political, and peremptory, Ellison suffered much black antagonism. He had written an exemplary book in every sense, had achieved it because writing was his life, his way to think. Art even for the best artists can be a fatality. Ellison was never so much alone as now, when political salvationists came everywhere out of the woodwork. As usual, telling "the Negro" what to think.

On December 12, 1987, the largest cathedral in North America, said to be the second largest in the world, St. John the Divine, in a mostly Hispanic neighborhood, Amsterdam Avenue at 110th Street, was filled to the rafters for the memorial service to James Baldwin. It was a wonderful sight in that extraordinary space—thousands of black and white New Yorkers sitting side by side in tribute to the Har-

lem-born Baldwin, an expatriate for many years, who in his early sixties had died in Paris of cancer.

The Episcopal church, once the richest and stuffiest church in New York, a tremendous landowner, has in this great cathedral certainly gone ecumenical with a vengeance. Jewish intellectuals are invited to address the congregation. There have been memorials to victims of the Holocaust. The plight of Central American Indians is luridly pictured just inside the entrance. You are made aware that at least on Amsterdam Avenue, in this magnificently oversized and perhaps never-to-be-finished cathedral (the Gothic design was approved in 1916), the church is trying to return to its roots among the poor, the *barrios,* the primitive, the easily overlooked, the dust of the earth. (God made man out of the dust of the earth.) In 1967 the bishop of New York announced that the cathedral might never be completed but would devote its energies to the poverty in the community surrounding it. Work was resumed in 1978, but the church cannot easily ignore its surroundings. You have to know the upper reaches of Amsterdam Avenue, where it is as yet ungentrified, to know how the other half lives.

Baldwin made history in the 1960s with *The Fire Next Time.* "God gave Noah the rainbow sign. No more water, the fire next time!" He had already, in *Nobody Knows My Name: More Notes of a Native Son,* shown what a blazing moral authority a black writer possessed—if he had the talent of James Baldwin. Edmund Wilson had been bowled over by Baldwin's essays, said he had never read another black writer so gifted. Perhaps, like admirers of Baldwin's first novel, *Go Tell It on the Mountain,* which took off from Baldwin's experience as a boy preacher out of school hours in a small revivalist church,

Wilson would have found Baldwin's later novels just as talented as his essays, but strained. Baldwin again and again sought to bring within the focus of a single novel the family and sexual discords that tore at him as much as did American racism.

Baldwin was as troubled a man as Richard Wright, as easily set ajar as Ralph Ellison. But he was younger, sassier, more urban and worldly-wise. He was a New Yorker—bred not only in Harlem, but by a good old-fashioned New York public high school, where he had active relationships with Jewish friends before moving on to Greenwich Village.

Baldwin was an irascible, constantly challenging, fascinating man. He thought of himself as homely, and in company gave the impression of daring you to think better of his looks than he did. He was quick, lively, endlessly witty, campy and hostile in the same measure. As with the emotional complexities of his later fiction, which kept me on edge but fascinated me by its grieving search for a way out, Baldwin in person was there yet not there. You never knew what was first in his mind as he entertained you —to remain the life of the party or to put you down. Race was always between us. You knew why it was so, but carefully wondered at times if it had to be there *all* the time.

Baldwin kept an apartment on New York's West Side for years. I lived in the next building, but never saw him. It was in Paris, in the 1950s, when he had begun his long love affair with France, that I saw him at all. He knew his way around, he enjoyed the innumerable gaffes and frustrations that came with being "an American in Paris." He stood out, a most charming personage. Whatever he was for his French intimates, he was for American friends a godsend. One day, as we were discussing the new, very

Jewish magazine that had just been set up in New York, *Commentary,* Baldwin challenged us to come up with sporty titles for articles. And immediately won, hands down, with "A Negro Looks at Henry James."

I could never think of Baldwin as an apostle to the Gentiles—meaning whites. *The Fire Next Time* was magnificent stuff to take over practically the whole issue of *The New Yorker* for November 17, 1962, especially when you pursued Baldwin's burning exposé against ads for magnificent silks, perfume and Caribbean resorts. But raging and telling as it all was, it was a performance. I never thought him interested in politics. So, sitting in that great interracial crowd in St. John the Divine, it was with some irony that I heard Amiri Baraka (Le Roi Jones) shout that Baldwin's writing came out of "a revolutionary mouth." Baraka blasted and thundered, the music was extraordinary, the "mixed" congregation glorious to be in. There is no doubt that for many black folk there, a *leader had died.*

The magnificent turnout "for Jimmy" was certainly a far cry from the description I was to read in the *Times* of his Harlem at the holiday season.

Bathed in the amber of the street lamps, the street is sepia-toned, sere. But the specter of drugs hangs over all who live here. It grips this street and subdues the Christmas spirit as evening falls. Daily skirmishes on drugs between the "straight life" people and the young and hungry. They vie for the sidewalks, for the vestibules and hallways of their homes, even for the street lights.

Young people clad in oversized jackets— sometimes girls, most often boys—saunter up and down the street, acting on signals they receive through electronic pagers at their hips. Other teen-agers zoom up and down the street in Volvo 760 turbos and Suzuki Samurais, which seem to be the cars of choice for drug dealers on the block.

There are six street lights on this block—three on each side of the street, staggered to provide the widest possible light cover. On summer-autumn nights, drug dealers keep themselves covered in darkness during the peak hours of the drug trade. The city has sent workers to repair lights on this block seven times this year, four times to the same section, the eastern end of 119th Street close to Fifth Avenue.

Last summer, in the peak months, a steady stream of people flowed into the block from dusk to dawn to get their drugs. They arrived in yellow cabs, on bicycles, in BMW's with N.J. license plates, and went to a small town house near a storefront church, to a series of basement apartments in brownstones, to first-floor apartments in one of the block's larger buildings.

Police raided drug sites almost every day and led several men out in chains and handcuffs. The dealers returned to the block within a week. As quickly as a malfunctioning light was repaired, its wires were cut or spliced again.

ALONE IN THE CITY

Closer yet I approach you,
What thought you have of me
now, I had as much of you—I
laid in my stores in advance,
I consider'd long and seriously
of you before you were born.

—*Walt Whitman*
"Crossing Brooklyn Ferry"

In darkest Brooklyn during the depression —and how well Bernard Malamud caught the wintry smudge as the light falls at year's end—the grocer Morris Bober, who is not old but has been made to feel so, is failing, dying, ending. He is so overwhelmed by failure that he can say only what is forced out of him at the end of his tether. "He was Morris Bober and could be nobody more fortunate. With that name you had no sure sense of property, as if it were in your blood and history not to possess, or if by some miracle to own something, to do so on the verge of loss."

Morris wearily forces himself out of bed at dawn in order to lug in the heavy milk cases. Soon he will sell the "Poileshe" an onion roll for three cents. Morris, his wife Ida and their daughter Helen address each other in a style so toneless that the words seem wrung out of them. Such bitterly laconic remarks, soliloquies really, are characteristic of Malamud's bitterly simple style in *The Assistant*. When life gets so reduced, language follows. These people are up against the wall. Each word may be their last. "Why do I cry? I cry for the world. I cry for my life that it went away wasted. I cry for you—." Helen: "I want a larger and better life, I want the return of my possibilities." In the subway, reading *Don Quixote*, she meets one of the young men whose function it is to disappoint her. "He was cordial but as usual held back something—his future."

Morris Bober, the depression period personified, was totally out of the rat race. In *Seize the Day*, Saul Bellow's Tommy Wilhelm in affluent postwar America has nothing else. He has nothing to live for but the chance, another chance, the main chance. He is still a dreamer for whom America as riches and success is the realest of illusions. Not particularly intelligent, or strong, or resourceful, he is particularly given to self-deception and inaccurate estimates of other people. He identifies himself with every new promise and delusion on the wing. With his blond, deceptively non-Jewish good looks, the routine unthinking line of chatter that has made him a successful salesman in the past, Tommy wearing a hat and smoking a cigar looks a part that on this day he no longer has the spirit to sustain.

New York in all its human weather is a constant register of Tommy's ups and downs. Bellow's great achievement was to show the imposition of force on people who are unable to recognize their true destiny until, at the end, the very end of their day, they are engulfed. Their bodies, when they are still young enough to be proud of them, are their only resistance to such force. Tommy, in his middle forties, has a heavy and strong back, "if already a little stooped or thickened." Maurice Venice, the agent: "His breath was noisy and his voice difficult and rather husky because of the fat in his throat." Bellow, who had some training in anthropology, is fond of such physical details; the body is the armor of the otherwise defenseless human person.

From the opening of *Seize the Day* we get the intensity of numbers on the West Side, the many old and impeded people, the anxious Jewish preoccupation with health—an allegory of survival as the central life problem. The physicality of every moment's experience is overwhelming. The ability to contend with life is everything.

Severe as these fictions were, they were full of the electric visual detail that only a great city provides. The *look* of New York is what at all times keeps the writer, artist, photographer, filmmaker in motion. It is the felt pulsation of crowds, the strange procession the great buildings make across the sky, the sudden almost shocking beauty of once humdrum streets in a violent rainstorm, the sudden grays and blacks like nothing seen before—or the moment after. It is being whisked in a taxi through Central Park through what T. S. Eliot called the "violet hour," when the great lights along the rim and the fading greenery within the park remind you of what a theater with endlessly shifting scenery you live in, of a performance that never stops, of people always "on."

In David Finn's gallery of people alone on the street, the matchless creativity of New York comes down in the end to some individual's depth of solitude that no one else in the crowd can fully gauge—one that is wholly *lived* without, perhaps, being fully known. Especially gifted as Finn is in catching the sculptural forms of buildings, terraces, lamp posts, fences in New York, he sees with a distinct purity the unseeing boy and his dog on the edge of the East River under Brooklyn Bridge, the Hispanic boy in his American summer regalia with the marked-up, *mucked*-up political graffiti on the wall behind him (the words changed to an ad from WORKERS LIBERATION TO REFRIGERATION), the hot dog vendors, the young lovers, the many "soldiers of summer" on park benches eating junk food and sipping from bottles and cans.

What I find most striking in Finn's photographs of lone individuals and small groups is the lack of strain in their faces. New York's tabloid violence is remarkably absent here. Even when Finn catches in front of the Port Authority Bus Terminal an open fight between a taxi driver and a passerby, the scrappers come out looking bemused, too absorbed *in* their intensity to show us the violence itself.

All this I consider a tribute to some underlying sense of harmony in Finn himself and his feeling for composition. A sense of their own inwardness, reflectiveness, musing is uppermost in these photographs. It is not that they are "at ease," though they look it, but that they are entirely caught up in some undisclosable part of *themselves*. As we are, without our fully knowing it. The five persons sitting on a Broadway island off One-hundredth Street, three men and two women, all as "ordinary" as can be except for the color in one man's cap, the bare chest and smart little chin beard of another—these folks do not even see each other, have plainly nothing to say to each other. But each is sunk in his or her *Existenz*. Just living, seeing and hearing nothing but the fact that they are, just at this moment, perilously alive.

On the evening of October 27, 1979, David Finn's brother Herbert, a civil rights lawyer in Phoenix, Arizona, was shot to death in the quiet residential neighborhood of Riverdale while sitting in David's car with his wife and David's wife and sister. Along with David's daughter, they had been to the opera. While they were waiting for David to return from seeing his daughter to her apartment, three young men held up the car, took the handbags from the women and Herbert's wallet. When Herbert made a move to retrieve his credit cards he was shot dead with a single .22 caliber bullet. He was to have left the next day for Egypt and Israel. The murderers mailed the credit cards back to David's wife.

Herbert had long wanted to write a book about New York. In a sense this book is a memorial to him.

A little after noon, April 30, 1976, a wonderful forty-nine-year-old family doctor, Walter Blumenson, was murdered while having a

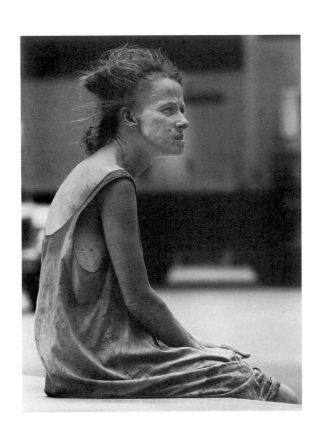

picnic lunch with a hospital coworker in Lincoln Terrace Park. I knew Dr. Blumenson, I certainly knew Lincoln Terrace Park. He was stabbed to death by what the paper referred to as knife-wielding thugs (*thugs* was still in currency). They robbed him of $200 and fled on foot. Neither Dr. Blumenson nor his companion offered any resistance, but the doctor objected verbally and was stabbed fatally in the chest.

One of the assailants was about seventeen, the other about eighteen. As I knew Dr. Blumenson, I knew the grassy knoll in the park at President Street and Rochester Avenue, a park where at sixteen I learned to smoke and to delight in the most advanced girl of the neighborhood. Dr. Blumenson sometimes worked up to eighteen hours a day, making house calls, caring for patients in the hospital, keeping office hours that were officially 5:00 to 8:00 P.M. but frequently lasted till midnight and later. "Until the last patient went home," as one put it.

Dr. Blumenson was married, the father of a nineteen-year-old son, Steve. Licensed in 1963, he had practiced in Brooklyn since that time.

His wife Anita learned of her husband's murder later in the day. "It happens every day, but it's always to the next person. Today I came home and found two policemen who told me my husband was dead. That's all I can say."

On November 8, 1987, the body of Ida Salzman, ninety-two years old, weighing ninety pounds, was found savagely beaten to death in the two-story brick house at 979 Hopkinson Avenue, between Lott and Hegemann avenues, where Mrs. Salzman had lived for the past sixty-eight years. She had been murdered four days before. She used to say that her husband Jacob had built their home and that she would stay there forever.

"She fought like a dog," said a police captain, who noted that the intruder apparently broke through three doors.

Two of my closest friends lived on Hopkinson between Lott and Hegemann. I passed Mrs. Salzman's house any week.

David Finn and his wife were interrogated by police all through the night of his brother's murder. When they reached home at 5:30 A.M., he couldn't stop shivering, though he wasn't cold, and kept repeating, "I can't believe it." The image of his brother slumped in the back seat would not leave his mind, nor would the words "I can't believe it."

Which formed the only response my head could make. In those hours I learned what it meant to be unable to accept reality. The cruel killing of my brother had earned me a special privilege to be absolved from the affairs of the world. I was surrounded by a hushed silence, broken only if I took the initiative . . . .

Twelve days after the murder, three black teenagers were apprehended. A few days later, a fourth. Their ages were nineteen, seventeen, seventeen and fifteen. Three of the young men came from middle-class homes in Mount Vernon and had no previous records.

As I struggled to regain my perspective on life, which I found extremely difficult, I felt no desire for revenge towards those who had killed my brother. I was heartbroken, shattered by the loss, and I knew I would never get over seeing him dead . . . .But hatred towards those who committed the murder offered no solace. Yet dying from a bullet fired by a young man who felt no compunction about taking the life of another human being carried a message of its own. It was a wound in the soul of man, and each person who was touched by it felt the scar in his or her being.

A truly remarkable police officer, Anthony Bouza, who had retired as chief of police in the Bronx . . . , a friend of mine, spoke to me with compassion and wisdom about my brother. He believes crime is a cancer which will destroy our society unless we get at its root causes—poverty and unemployment. My father, a criminologist, had written books in the 1930s and 1940s stating a similar point of view. Chief Bouza feels that the problem has become explosive since my father wrote his books. The isolation of the poor in our cities has created pressures which are intolerable. People who can't speak the language, can't find jobs and can't find decent places to live in are excluded from society—then desperation overwhelms morality and law.

. . . The men arrested for the murder of my brother are from good families in middle-class communities. The cancer originates in those burned-out buildings, the piles of rubble and decay, those impoverished populations I saw as I traveled from precinct to precinct in the South Bronx. It is now metastasizing to the rest of the community.

Chief Bouza is an optimist. He believes in America . . . a giant who is too busy to hear the cries of pain from the little people at his feet. But as the pain gets . . . louder, the giant will do what needs to be done to cure the disease.

One of the most remarkable photographs in our book testifies beyond all words to David Finn's grief and shock, his spiritual desolation following the murder of his brother. The branches of a tree are shown so gnarled and twisted about each other that they form a barrier to the cool whiteness of the building on the left and the venerable and ornamentally interesting building with French windows opening onto balconies. At the moment there is no way out. The heart is at a standstill. There is no way of knowing what another feels in the horror, disbelief and terror of coming upon a brother murdered.

To really get the full flavor of the city's daily allotment of burglary, robbery, assault, rape, arson, murder, you have to peruse with patience section B of the *New York Times*. On the day that a wise man in Wall Street gloated that there had not been such an increase in wealth since the Renaissance, one could also read that a twenty-six-year-old resident of Torrington, Connecticut, who was in New York City on his way to Washington for a job interview, died after he was stripped and chased onto the tracks in Times Square by a jeering mob of youths and vagrants. His family said he had been terrorized, having been robbed twice in twenty-four hours and stripped of his clothes, suitcase and money. With a mob following him he jumped onto the tracks of the Flushing line. As a police officer tried to have the power shut off, the man shoved his hands against the electrified third rail, fell backward, cried out and died a few minutes later.

An elderly couple who were assaulted and robbed in their Bronx apartment hanged themselves in their bedroom after leaving a note saying, "We don't want to live in fear any more." The couple—Hans Kable, seventy-eight years old and his wife Emma, seventy-six—had laid out their best clothes on the bed of their neatly furnished apartment at 275 East 168th Street. Detectives of the Police Senior Citizens Robbery Unit said that the couple had been robbed early the month before, when Mr. Kable returned from shopping. As the elderly man reached the door of his fourth-floor apartment he was rushed from behind and fell to the floor inside. The robber then went through his pockets and removed his wallet with its contents—$2.

Leonard Mitchell of 1165 Grand Avenue, the Bronx, twenty years old, pleaded guilty in State

Supreme Court to having raped a woman in her apartment after he trailed firemen who were fighting a blaze nearby. Unable to get at the fire because the apartment windows were barred, the firemen then went up to the roof to fight the blaze. The defendant meanwhile entered the apartment, robbed and raped the woman. Her cries for help finally brought the firemen, who subdued him.

Murder and manslaughter accelerated in New York City in the summer, headed for a new record, according to Police Department statistics. If it continues at the current rate, the figures will definitely challenge the all-time high, said Deputy Chief Alan H. Hoehl. The July murder-manslaughter statistics brought the total number of people who died violent deaths at the hands of criminals to 1,030 in the first seven months of the year, 10.9% more than in the same period in 1987.
New York Times, October 27, 1988

Most of the city's troubles stem from the presence of persons whose everyday actions make life hazardous for those around them. No one predicted the emergence of this kind of conduct, nor did anyone foresee that it would take such destructive proportions. . . . If the number of addicts, derelicts and other undesirables diminishes over the coming generation, their disappearance will stem not from well-wrought laws or intelligent administration, but rather from new combinations of events which produce new patterns of conduct. . . . Each year the city comes on more strongly as a center of consumption while its productive counterweight grows lighter.
Andrew Hacker, *The New Yorkers* (1975)

These people will not be satisfied with a very slow, modest improvement of their condition, but insist that the improvement be substantial and swift. The previous immigrants to our cities would have thought such a demand presumptuous; they were resigned to poverty in their own lifetime and placed their hopes for improvement with their children and grandchildren. This kind

of resignation is going out of fashion everywhere in the world."
Irving Kristol, "It's Not Such a Bad Crisis to Live In"
New York Times, May 8, 1967

The number of poor people has increased dramatically in the last decade. Hospitals are overwhelmed as poor in NYC search for care. The poor as defined by the Federal government have risen from 15% (1975) to 24% in 1988. The near absence of primary care in many areas: the Director of the City's Health System Agency says many people "have never been to see a doctor for any preventive care or screening." The poorest and weakest New Yorkers now flood emergency rooms, relying on them for everything from asthma attacks to treatment of chronic illnesses.
New York Times, December 4, 1988

In a vast new housing complex on newly gentrified Columbus Avenue a significant number of tenants are blacks, decidedly not of the underclass. Any morning I am not too caught up in this book to walk my wife, Judith, to the subway off Central Park West, we find ourselves in the company of physicians, museum people, "coordinators," "consultants," systems analysts, programmers. They are in banks, television, computers, publishing, the community colleges, the ballet. And no matter how early I get to my typewriter, I can see some very fast doubles games going on across the street.

I know nothing about the young blacks right across from us, the blacks getting in and out of some splendid cars in the parking lot, the head of the tenants' association who never walks out without leading two poodles, one black and the other white. This vast assemblage of indistinguishable buildings, owned by the most publicity-conscious landlord in town, is an island of enlightenment. What a difference a modicum of economic security makes! The only time I heard voices raised here—a scream of despair in the middle of the night—was in the very next apartment, soon vacated by the man who could not meet his rent. That lonely cry makes me think of all the street blacks I see talking to themselves, and the black whom David Finn observed perched on a pediment of the central Brooklyn Public Library. He was dressed for action, yet was poised on the pediment like a dancer awaiting his next step.

Two blocks away from my house, on Broadway, there is a daily carnage. Drunks outside the single-room-occupancy hotel dazedly eye me as I make my way past mounds of glass, hills of garbage, blacks comatose on the pavement, blacks playing craps at eight in the morning in front of the hydrant that for several years now has been so battered and assaulted—the cover disappeared a long time ago—that in the hottest summer weather it gives off only a trickle. On good old Broadway the river of life is at its flood, thick and angry with bodies jostling one another every which way so that it is no wonder you and you and you no longer see the young black with chin beard who used to wait outside the bakery wistfully helping to turn the revolving door as you left. He now resides on the pavement where people wait in line to obtain day-old bread. I think he has given up.

The competition is certainly intense. Between One-hundredth Street and the subway at Ninety-sixth, I was stopped by five beggars to the block. A few were black, others by now of an indeterminate color. By no means did all present the necessary face of intense pain and wretchedness. There is now some indiscriminate and openly cynical holding out of the paper cup. Last year's medieval look of abject cripples and lepers has here and there been replaced by a snarling smile that openly says, "C'mon, you bastard with someplace to go, give!"

A young woman sits at the top of the subway stairs. One hand and one leg are loosely wrapped in bandages. Her refrain: "I have an advanced cancer." More and more there is no story to grab you, just a hand holding out a soiled paper cup. Say what you like about them. The *presence* of so many people on the street, many living there, at rest even in winter on the pavement under your feet, is the "story." There is nothing you can say, guess, detest about them that is as important as the fact that when you come out of a train in Grand Central Station, a dozen blacks are lying against a wall, all of them asleep next to the plastic garbage sacks holding their worldly belongings. You have to shake your head when you look into beautiful St. Bartholomew's Church on Park Avenue and see a dozen or so cots right inside the entrance. "Sanctuary" for the night. But in the day?

"New York is just a failure," says the columnist Murray Kempton, one of the few 1930s radicals who has kept his edge, his sense of outrage. Even in eighteenth-century New York Tom Paine grieved that affluence and wretchedness side by side made him think of the living and dead chained together. The thought of *New York* as a "failure" is not common just now. The problem of the street people is how "to dispose of them." Like other forms of waste, they may be "a danger to our health." If there are to be many more of them, they will seriously impede traffic.

On a beautiful starlit night before Christmas 1987, on East Fifty-second Street off Fifth Avenue, outside the entrance to Cartier's where a holiday party was in progress, a man was lying face down on the pavement. A frolic-

some, excited-looking couple in evening dress got out of a limousine and approached the party. The lady positively gleaming in her fur, the man excessively bald for his years but looking proprietary, rich, assured. The lady suddenly removed her fur and handed it with a negligent gesture to her companion, who ran with it down the street to his limousine and chauffeur. If the lady had looked splendid enough in her fur, she was now lit up like the proverbial Christmas tree as she stood there at the entrance to Cartier's, a body right at her feet, awaiting her companion and their proud entrance to the party.

If "New York is just a failure," a great many people who regard themselves as the city's leaders and shining examples certainly don't believe this. The "hottest people, the success people," as Donald Trump calls them, share with Norman Mailer a pride that New York is "the greatest city in the world, the most magnificent, most creative, most just, dazzling, bewildering and planned of cities." There is something familiar about them, a democratic amiability that they share with politicians. They are always "nice" and on call, as modest to the outward look as people less accomplished and celebrated —only richer, thinner, and clearly more significant. There is an aura. When the Rainbow Room atop the RCA building was reopened for a private party in 1987, in its dazzling space of spaces on the sixty-fifth floor, David Rockefeller (his father John D., Jr., created Rockefeller Center) said he had invited "people we thought are important in New York today." These came to seven hundred people, distributed over two nights of festivities.

The guest list at the official opening in 1935 included Astors, Auchinclosses, Roosevelts, Burdens and Phillipses. Such names were a link, even in 1935, to "old New York," to the aristocratic diarist of New York life George Templeton Strong, Mayor Philip Hone, Police Commissioner Theodore Roosevelt, mayors of New York like Seth Low, George B. McClellan, William J. Gaynor, John Purroy Mitchell. In 1845 one Moses Yale Beach actually published a book listing *Wealthy Citizens of New York*. But for decades the "important" New Yorkers, whose residences were within a narrow circle, were the men of letters Washington Irving and Bayard Taylor, the *Tribune* editor Horace Greeley, the political eminences Chester A. Arthur and Samuel J. Tilden, the enlightened capitalist (and inventor) Peter Cooper and his son-in-law Abram S. Hewitt. But then came the "swells," who had the money with which to force their way into "good society." Who now remembers that the social leader August Belmont, a pillar of the Democratic party, was born Schoenberg in the Rhineland, arrived in the New World as agent of the Rothschilds?

In 1987 there was no questioning the importance of Donald Trump, who swept into the Rainbow Room with his wife Ivana and approved the decor. "Nice job," he said. "Understated." An almost equally prominent real estate mogul, Leona Helmsley, seemed mesmerized by the skyline. "How do you like my husband's buildings?" she asked, pointing out the window as a cocktail pianist played "This Nearly Was Mine." Among the seven hundred: the much-admired philanthropist Brooke Astor. Ex-mayor John V. Lindsay. The powerful theater owner and producer James Nederlander. The "television personality" Barbara Walters. *The New Yorker's* Brendan Gill. Estée Lauder. Liza Minnelli and Mikhail Baryshnikov. The dress designer Pauline Trigère and the choreographer Tommy Tune.

Music and flowers were everywhere. Waiters were in snappy aubergine outfits, maîtres d'hotel in champagne-colored tails. The number of people who have always been in love with the Rainbow Room precluded the idea of a sit-down dinner. It was announced that when open to the public, the Rainbow Room would be "a people-friendly environment in the style of the twenty-first century."

Donald Trump likes to describe himself as "only a boy from Queens." He has been hailed by a friendly publicity man as "one kind of quintessential New Yorker. He's the kid with a smile and a shine who looks like he's selling the Brooklyn Bridge, only it turns out he owns it." Donald Trump, the man who would like to own *everything*. The Grand Hyatt Hotel. Trump Tower, the sixty-eight-story retail and commercial building. Trump Parc, fifty-eight stories, 350 condominium units. The Plaza Hotel. The Trump Plaza Motel and Casino in Atlantic City. Trump Plaza of the Palm Beaches. Resorts International in Atlantic City, of which he owns 12 percent equity and 88.1 percent voting control. This includes the 120,000-square-foot Taj Mahal Casino in Atlantic City now under construction and three hotels with 1,400 rooms in the Bahamas. He just sold the St. Moritz in New York but has acquired the Eastern Airlines Shuttle.

On a grubby, torrid August day in 1988, a crowd collected at the foot of Thirtieth Street and East River to stare in proper humility and wonder at a wonderfully sleek, shiningly white 300-foot yacht. The man whose name is already attached to a tower, a castle, a plaza and a parc had now given it to a princess. *Trump Princess!* Leading a press party of sixty reporters and cam-

eramen around his latest acquisition, Trump contentedly informed them that it accommodated twenty-two passengers, a crew of thirty-one, contained an operating room, a discotheque, 210 telephones, marbled lavatories. "There's never been anything like it in terms of quality, which is what I like, of course," said Trump, stroking a padded suede wall during the tour. In one of eight double suites, he pressed a button that slowly spun a worked metal column. "This is a good sculpture, which you want of course. But behind it is the TV and stereo and VCR, which you want but don't want to see."

Trump bought the yacht from the sultan of Brunei, who had secured it as collateral for a multimillion-dollar loan to the Saudi Arabian entrepreneur Adnan M. Khashoggi. After a six-month $10-million refitting in the Netherlands, the *Trump Princess* entered New York harbor for the first time in her present incarnation. "Donald really stressed the charitable aspects of the yacht," said Tom Gates, a reporter for the *West Side Spirit* and *Palm Beach Social Pictorial*. He explained that the yacht would be used for fund-raising parties. "Donald said he felt pangs of guilt sometimes at owning a boat like this," the reporter admitted. "But he shouldn't. He makes his money legally, after all."

Speaking for himself, Trump added that ownership of the yacht is a form of patriotism. "This country has been taken advantage of by every country in the world, especially our allies, like Japan, Kuwait and Saudi Arabia. So I look at this ship as one of the great jewels of the world, and as an American I'm proud to have pulled it back here. This yacht was considered a jewel, the jewel of Monte Carlo; and I think Americans should have the jewels, should go out and buy the jewels of the world, because we're a great country."

In the crowd gathered in front of the *Trump Princess* was a slim, lithe blonde in a light summer dress staring open-mouthed at the yacht. It was a thing of beauty, of very great beauty. On that suffocatingly hot day, the *Princess* shone above the industrial grime and heedless traffic like the most improbable, immaculate swan. The blonde looked and looked, then walked out of her dress and in her bikini underwear presented herself at the foot of the gangplank, looking straight at the astonished members of the crew.

His Honor Edward I. Koch, three times elected mayor of New York, has in his own way had this gift for making himself the center of attention. Since municipal politics in New York resembles nothing more subtle than hand-to-hand combat with stone axes, Koch's presentation of self lacked Woody Allen's ready sense of irony. Koch had made his way up, up, up from the ranks of just another New York congressman. He had been a Reform Democrat in Greenwich Village, had marched in Selma, and at social occasions when I first saw him, before he attained his present persona, actually seemed more diffident than not.

Other times, other manners. Ed Koch discovered he had a mouth that could not be stopped by any occasion. Wherever he appeared, he gave the public everything he had, everything he was. He was the public personage and "major player" in New York least capable of keeping a secret. What you see is what you get, Koch said in effect. He threw himself upon New York as if he had no life except the one he was publicly leading. He blurted out everything he thought and felt like a bar mitzvah boy sure of being applauded for his big confirmation

speech, endlessly loved by his own family. Appealing to his own people as equally *arriviste* and happy with the status quo, he sensed that the politics of familiarity—"How'm I doing, folks?"—would work with others. The old immigrant and blue-collar class had become smug in its present prosperity. It had not lost its brashness, its bitter recollection of old slights, its fear and resentment of the destitute, the derelicts, the muggers, and quite a few blacks.

Koch combined the New York *alrightnik*'s new conservatism with an aggressiveness clearly founded in psychology. Even if you are repressed, never show it in public. Politics even in New York had never before been so tied up with the crudest egotism as when Ed Koch became mayor. Once, when asked in what guise he would like to come back to earth, he promptly replied, "As me." Though he was becoming a favorite of the big real estate developers, he managed by the sheer crudity of his public manners to give off the suggestion that he was ever and forever one of the city's people, a populist at heart.

Perhaps it was some remnant of childhood innocence that explained why Koch was mocked but not blamed when the crookedness of so many political associates surfaced in January 1986. The borough president of Queens, Donald Manes, killed himself. The head of the Bronx Democratic machine was indicted on federal racketeering, conspiracy and mail-fraud charges for illegally using his influence to sell portable computers to the city's Parking Violations Bureau. Several agencies, especially the one concerned with the health inspection of restaurants, were accused of extortion. The Housing Authority, the Department of Environmental Protection, the Department of General Services, the Board of Education, the Taxi and Limousine Commission all presented examples of wrongdoing. Koch: "No section of our society is without corruption. You can't prevent the fact that there is corruption. Our job is to apprehend those engaged in it." Koch's close friend, the city's Cultural Affairs Commissioner Bess Myerson, a former Miss America, went on trial for allegedly persuading a judge to lower the alimony being paid by Miss Myerson's lover, Carl (Andy) Capasso. Capasso, a contractor who had benefited from $150 million worth of city sewer contracts in recent years, was just then in the federal penitentiary. He set up a new corporation after his conviction and was still raking in money from city contracts.

The "big players," as they were admiringly described in stories about the millions piled on millions that were being made from four million square feet of skyscrapers usurping sun and air, were the developers. In one breathtaking deal after another they were in effect taking over the city with thirty- and fifty-story towers in the middle of residential neighborhoods. Philip K. Howard, director of the Municipal Art Society and of New York's Industrial Development Agency, complained, "New York is becoming a city we don't want." He pointed out that light and air were declining in direct proportion to the rise in congestion on the streets and sidewalks and that the new projects, without relation to anything else, would interrupt the continuous walls of storefronts that for a century and a half have successfully provided the framework for New York's retail commerce.

Seasoned city watchers and architecture critics like Brendan Gill of *The New Yorker* expressed dismay that while City Hall just wanted to maximize revenue, it proudly fostered huge new projects that capitalized on the city's neighborhoods without noticing or caring that new developments like parasites were systematically leeching all the character from local communities. Residential enclaves like Murray Hill and Carnegie Hill found themselves invaded by blockbuster projects with fancy names that resembled nothing so closely as inflated versions of 1930s public housing. Neighborhoods along First and Third Avenues, the Upper East Side, were victimized by towers separated from the sidewalk and the rest of the community by cold, useless plazas. The area south of Lincoln Center was developed not as a neighborhood but as unconnected apartment towers exceeding fifty stories that did not offer even the pretext of fitting into the fabric of the surrounding areas. The waterfront was not being integrated with neighborhoods like those along Riverside Drive. It just reflected the unconnected towers of Jersey City and Fort Lee in New Jersey.

Literature has been known to thrive on the disparities within society, the lurid contrasts and violent contradictions that give so much color and narrative strength to the social novel in Balzac and such nineteenth-century masters. New York today is marked by such extremes high and low, delirious consumption and constant menace, cultural frippery and undeclared race war that a keen observer like Tom Wolfe can almost be forgiven for invoking "my idol Balzac" when pushing *The Bonfire of the Vanities.* Or turning himself, Tom Wolfe from Richmond, Virginia, Yale Ph.D. in American Studies, into such a florid character and publicity genius. Mark Twain, who also wore white winter and summer, would have been impressed by Wolfe's *seven* white suits, if not by his boast, "Those are real buttonholes on the jacket sleeves." It is difficult to escape one's environment even when one is satirizing it.

The Bonfire of the Vanities is an impishly observed *tour d'horizon* of New York, late eighties, at its wildest and most reportable. As Wolfe says, "I decided first on the setting. I figured the characters would walk into the setting once I had it framed in my mind." The setting is everything for an author describing himself as a "status theorist," heavily influenced by the great sociologist Max Weber. Wolfe "couldn't believe that nobody else was writing about this in book form somewhere . . . the astounding prosperity generated by the investment banking industry and the racial and ethnic animosity."

Everyone gets it in *Bonfire,* since on Wolfe's terms New York is a thoroughly greedy, dissolute, cynical, exploitable society; and no doubt everyone *should*. Balzac would have been surprised to learn that *everybody* in New York is equally awful. Balzac looked behind the misdeeds of a purely economic civilization to a loftier time. He lavished his deepest consideration on characters capable of self-sacrifice. No such souls apparently exist in New York. If some did, they would never escape the net of Wolfe's tightly woven reportage. He is mesmerized by social types, representatives of every purlieu, specimens of local speech habits. But then no other novelist in years, least of all a southerner, has devoted so many pages to the Bronx—to say nothing of its "fortress-like" courthouse and the unbelievable sight of black defendants in a patrol wagon and a Jewish judge outside its doors screaming the vilest racial insults at each other.

Bonfire is all-too specialized to have lasting interest. Wolfe reflects the passion for exposure that is the life of the media and has become the fashionable New York climate, along with the derision that replaces intelligence in a society so closely packed. The trouble with employing representative types is that their surface traits become everything, turn them into cartoons.

Nobody could turn a man like Donald Trump into a great fictional capitalist like Frank Algernon Cowperwood in Dreiser's *The Financier* and *The Titan*. Marianne Moore said in a poem on the fur district, "It's not the plunder but the accessibility to experience." That is a thought too deep for the characters now occupying New York novels. Even they talk of the "bottom line." Novels about human beings— even the young kind—were no longer just *set* in New York. They had to be still another New York model—a commodity derisive but cheerless, special to New York like *New York* magazine and the cosmetic counters at Bloomingdale's. Some kind of last resort. An arresting moment in Christopher Knowlton's *Real World:* "Doesn't it scare you that you may live here and do pretty much what we do today until the day you retire, and the only difference will be you eat in better restaurants?"

In Jay McInerney's *Bright Lights, Big City* the city consists not of individuals but of tribes, as in the *Bonfire of the Vanities*. The antagonism and suspicion with which our provincial lad sees one conspicuous New York tribe are touching because of *his* utter vacancy, which of course feels like homelessness.

The car is full of Hasidim from Brooklyn— gnomes in black with briefcases full of diamonds. You take a seat beside one of them. He is reading from the Talmud, running his finger across the page. The strange script is similar to the graffiti signatures all over the surface of the subway car, but the man does not look up at the graffiti, nor does he try to steal a peek at the headlines of your *Post*. This man has a God and

a History, a Community. He has a perfect economy of belief in which pain and loss are explained in terms of a transcendental balance sheet, in which everything works out in the end and death is not really death. Wearing black wool all summer must seem like a small price to pay. He believes he is one of God's chosen, whereas you feel like an integer in a random series of numbers. Still, what a fucking haircut . . . .

Sometimes you feel like the only man in the city without group affiliation . . . .

It was around this time—the "gaudy, impatient eighties"—that someone on Wall Street announced that the city had just seen the greatest creation of wealth since the sixteenth century. A lot of this "wealth" was to disappear in still another October crash, but the fascination with wealth was so great that on occasion it extended to the wealthy. At least one genuinely talented writer—Truman Capote—had even before the Age of Trump come to identify every inch of his sensibility with the very very rich in New York. The "scandalous" unfinished novel he left at his death in 1984, *Answered Prayers,* was, he maintained, a contemporary equivalent of Proust's masterpiece and "would examine the small world of the very rich—part aristocratic, part café society—of Europe and the east coast of the United States." Writing chapters out of sequence, he boasted, "I was able to do this only because the plot—or rather plots—was true, and all the characters were real; it wasn't difficult to keep it all in mind, for I hadn't invented anything." Apparently this made it more difficult for Capote to publish. He developed a severe writer's block. After all, he was on the phone to his characters half the day, never tired of exchanging gossip, used his own letters and journals for "a book I had long been planning: a

variation on the nonfiction novel."

As *Answered Prayers* was postponed year after year, Capote became impatient and published four sections of his manuscript in *Esquire.* "La Côte Basque," an inordinately bitchy account of ladies belonging to a very special set lunching on their intimates, as it were, produced an explosion that rocked this very small society Capote had set out to describe. "Virtually every friend he had in this world ostracized him for telling thinly disguised tales out of school, and many of them never spoke to him again." Capote: "What did they expect? I'm a writer, and I use everything. Did all those people think I was just there to entertain them?"

The most genuine, most deeply felt fragments of *Answered Prayers* dealt not with the super-rich but the seaminess of West Forty-second Street. Capote "knew" the rich only as a kind of pet, a gifted and wickedly charming writer whose deepest preoccupations were as marginal as he came to look. "Being a friend of the rich, making a living out of it," says one character in the book about another who is a sort of whore to the rich, "one day of that is harder than a month's work of twenty niggers working on a chain gang." But describing Forty-second west of Seventh, Capote went to town, all right:

. . . a movie at one of those ammonia-scented all-night movie palaces. It was after one when I set out, and the route of my walk carried me along nine blocks of Eighth Avenue. Prostitutes, blacks, Puerto Ricans, a few whites and indeed all strata of street-people society—the luxurious Latin American pimps (one wearing a white mink hat and a diamond bracelet), the heroin-nodders nodding in doorways, the male hustlers, among the boldest of them gypsy boys and Puerto Ricans and runaway hillbilly rednecks no more than fourteen and fifteen years old ("Mister! Ten dollars! Take me home! Fuck me all night!") circled the sidewalks like buzzards above an abattoir. Then the occasional cruising cop car, its passengers uninterested, unseeing, having seen it all until their eyes are rheumy with the sight.

I passed the Loading Zone, an S & M bar at 40th and Eighth, and there was a gang of laughing, howling, leather-jacketed, leather-helmeted jackals surrounding a young man, costumed exactly as they were, who unconscious, was sprawled between the curb and the sidewalk, where all his friends, colleagues, tormentors, whatever the hell you cared to call them, were urinating on him, drenching him from head to heel.

By contrast with this unfortunate side of life, Capote at the tables of the very rich was glad to admit

there is at least one respect in which the rich, the really very rich, *are* different from other people. They understand *vegetables* . . . have you ever noticed how, in the homes of the very rich, . . . at Bunny and Babe's, they always serve only the most beautiful vegetables, and the greatest variety? The greenest *petits pois,* infinitesimal carrots, corn so baby-kerneled and tender it seems almost unborn, lima beans tinier than mice eyes, and the young asparagus! the limestone lettuce! the raw red mushrooms, zucchini! . . .

Alas, Truman, you did not make the "very very rich" as succulent as you did their teeny, teeny little vegetables, "tinier than mice eyes." All you did was to make the rich *scandalous.* To you these could only be scandals of the bedroom. Such private scandals, known to us only through the chain letters of gossip, no longer have class priority. They are assuredly duplicated behind the aluminum awnings of two-family houses in Long Island City, the old-law tenements left in the barrio off Amsterdam Avenue, the transient hotels off Broadway. Everybody's doin' it!

What makes the superrich interesting, if at all, is their money—and the labyrinthine ways in which much money makes more money. Since nothing else just now is as sacred as money, the very very rich are in a sense more sacred to themselves than other people can ever be to *their* selves. But that is a subtle climate of feeling not easily grasped from the size of the vegetables they serve.

POSTSCRIPT: WE ARE ALL HERE

The taxi taking us from the Upper West Side to the East Village, where a family party was celebrating the arrival of my wife's half-French grandson, was driven by a grumpy Jew from Moscow who snaked his way expertly around the packed holiday streets but with whom the only common language was each other's childhood Yiddish. The driver taking us back was a Czech whose name had been changed in France. The driver taking us in from the airport the other day was Haitian, very quick to assure us —who would ask him?—that he was *"pas illégal."* Returning from an Italian vacation on a plane crowded with Moroccan Jews whose English seems to be limited to "HIAS," the Hebrew Immigration and Aid Society, which, to his amazement, greeted my father on the pier when he arrived in 1907. I enjoy their crowding the windows as we float over the New York skyline. "Where Empire State Building? Where Statue Liberty? Where George Washington Bridge? Show us!"

The taxi drivers of New York fascinate me by their foreignness. Angels were first of all "messengers," and New York taxi drivers are no angels. Nevertheless, I think of them as "messengers," the peculiar links of the city to the world as they dash about, just in from Egypt, Rumania, India and Trinidad. I have been driven by Eskimos from Alaska, Israeli reserve officers taking an M.A. in art history at Columbia, Russian ex-gentry so old-fashioned that they opened the door for you on arrival, a Hasid wearing an overflowing beard, a wide fur hat and a satiny frock coat, an Iowa-born seminarian at Union Theological who could not locate Times Square. Just now there are lots of Sikhs.

Each had a story to tell, and since we were temporarily each other's prisoners, time in

which to tell it. And why is it that I always need to listen? I just can't get over New York as planet Earth's still-favorite shore of refuge, first port of call, New York as a Tower of Babel in which you don't even know what language is being spoken around you, much less what is being said. New York is one Latin American casbah after another into which are squeezed so many half-suffocated people that whole streets of the Upper West Side seem self-enclosed, impenetrable to the gringo, held together by fear and distrust. During the taking of the 1980 census, one hard-pressed official agreed with our apoplectic mayor that there *had* to be an undercount. "Most of the Dominicans on West 107th Street," he glumly reported, "don't understand English. It's an incredible, thriving subculture and they won't hesitate to say there are two or three people in their apartment when in the real world there are four, five, six. And this block isn't much different from many others in this area."

Every once in a while, surveying the massed Spanish-language dailies and weeklies on the newsstands, browsing among the fine Spanish bookstores on Fourteenth Street, hearing the repeated cry, *"Mira! Mira!"* from Puerto Ricans for whom the city will be forever new and strange, then remembering the unbelievable crush of people in Caracas and Mexico City, I think of the cold summing-up I heard in Rio de Janeiro from an *education* official: "We have more than a hundred million people in Brazil, most of whom we don't need."

Does New York "need" all our millions? Somehow the question never comes up. A grumpy and cruelly wide-meshed paternalism is more our style. The truth is that New York is a geographical expression for the wildest, zaniest experiment ever open to democracy on such a scale. New York represents the most extraordinary concentration of human beings, many of whom could never have been so wildly ambitious and so "successful" anywhere else. Nor so assertive, truculent, suspicious, violent. Striving continuously with and against each other, they make up a stupendous, dizzying, still improbable form of organization that is hardly a true city community but rather a league of different tribes, an Austro-Hungarian Empire in miniature, never really meshing but holding together because it must. And because the political structure and tradition of the United States will still not have it any other way.

It cannot be said of New York what Lyndon Johnson said of Miami—"not an American city." New York is a great American city, the greatest, such as only America could have fostered. In its giddy, daredevil, vaguely inhuman but still protective way, having taken in more people from all the rest of the world than any other American city, it embodies and even flaunts the headlong pace, the buoyancy, the sky's-the-limit quality so near to the American temper. New York is the Book of Numbers come back again, the inspiration and model of every kind of pictorial and literary inspiration. Its greatest native writer, Walt Whitman, said of his epic *Leaves of Grass* (a work inconceivable except by a New Yorker), "If anything can justify my revolutionary attempts and utterances it is such *ensemble*—like a great city to modern civilization & a whole combined clustering paradoxical unity, a man, a woman."

As American cities go, New York is a very old and even venerable city, once the national capital and still deep in American tradition. Its greatest traditions include its preeminence as a great world bridge, the most important link between Europe and the whole of America,

between North and South America, between different parts of North America, between New England and the southern states. And no other American city has been such a center for art and literature, drama and music, for publishing and world communications.

New York may very well be the biggest subject for American literature in our century. So of course it has inspired more chagrin, a subtler sense of tragedy, of displacement, homelessness, and nostalgia for easier places to live in, than any other city. The Michigan writer Jim Harrison in *Wolf: A False Memoir:* "The soiled light, even the summer sun never quite clear, the air smelling as if it had been sprayed with some chemical." Flannery O'Connor from Georgia in "Judgment Day": "The window looked out on a brick wall and down into an alley full of New York air, the kind fit for cats and garbage. Here she didn't even live in a house. She lived in a pigeon-hut of a building, with all stripes of foreigner, all of them twisted in the tongue. It was no place for a sane man." Jean-Paul Sartre from Paris: "New York is striped with parallel, incommunicable meanings. I walk among the small brick houses, the color of dried blood. They are younger than European houses, but because of their fragility they seem much older. . . . It occurs to me that New York is about to acquire a history, that it already has its ruins. This is to adorn with a little softness the harshest city in the world." Isaac Bashevis Singer from Warsaw, long a New Yorker but in imagination still European, has Masha, a survivor, sigh over New York in *Enemies: A Love Story:* "I miss the sight of green grass, a breath of fresh air. Even in the camps the air wasn't as polluted as it is here."

New York retains so much of the world's tragedies, its endless displacements and tragedies! Yet no one walking its streets with attention can miss some very deep truths of the human experience as the century of *les guerres en chaîne* rumbles to its end. So it is exciting to be a writer here, as it is fruitful for an artist-photographer to keep his eyes open. The subject never lets you off. There is so much humanity packed up in these streets, so much friction, so much idiocy, so much learning, artistry, appetite for living, so much crime and so much lovemaking, so much eating and drinking on the open street, that it is not altogether inhuman to shut our ears to the screams we hear in the night.

Too much, we say. It is much of the time all too much. Why should *we* have to confront this torrent of life, why should we have to confront all the injustice and suffering in the world just because we live in "the supreme metropolis"? But the clash of tongues, the tacit war between the tribes, the plethora of words and images pouring onto the many screens demanding to be looked at for basic information as well as "entertainment"—these all pose in the city the fascinating excessiveness of the human scene. In a great modern city everything is excessive;

human nature seems more demanding, more naturally unsatisfiable, inclined to destruction. How are writer and artist to do justice to the extraordinary spectrum of human life in the "greatest" city, to the endless clamor of "I want! I want!"—when the city arouses us with energy by which it exhausts us? How are writer and artist who are naturally part of this city scene, who have actually grown up with all this hardness—how are they to preserve their creative identity, their moral distance? How, in this atmosphere of excessive stimulation, are any of us to avoid being submerged in too powerful an environment?

In less than a single century Americans have lived through the rise and crisis of supercity. We learn to accept our lot, and even to enjoy it, by accepting endless contradictions. We recognize the comedy in so many ill-matched people packed together, the zaniness at the top and the bottom, above all the incessant play of human differences. And what a play it is. If our very saturation in the city made it possible to put our lives into this book, New York has shown us that not always a problem to be solved, it is an experience to be shared.

ABOUT THE PHOTOGRAPHS

Over a period of ten years I have taken thousands of photographs of New York for the book Alfred Kazin and I planned together— initially at the instigation of our mutual friend Harry Abrams, who introduced us to each other, and later under the guidance of Arthur Samuelson, our editor at Harper & Row, who helped us weave together our vision of the city.

For me this has been more of a grand idea than a project. We never had a list of places to be photographed, an outline of subjects to be covered, a plan of what would ultimately be the right collection for a book. My approach as the photographer was a very personal one, taking time out of a busy day to visit favorite haunts with my camera, spending hours in the dark-room working on prints, then going out to a different part of the city and back again to the darkroom; sometimes letting weeks go by without taking any photographs and at other times making a concentrated effort to take a whole series of photographs in a particular section or on a particular theme.

Most of the time I went by myself, with my Hasselblad and my assortment of lenses. I never worried about having a lot of equipment with me, and often (I suppose foolishly) left my bag standing unattended while I wandered about shooting whatever caught my eye. Most people didn't bother to take notice of me, and if they did it was usually with a friendly curiosity. Once in the South Bronx, while I was photo-graphing some wrecks of buildings, a woman shouted, "Are you taking pictures for the *News*? Show 'em how bad it looks! Maybe they'll do something about it."

One of my most prized tools was a 500-millimeter lens that I had acquired some years earlier in order to take detailed photographs of sculptures that were high up in churches and otherwise inaccessible to the camera eye without the benefit of a scaffold. It had been invaluable, for instance, when I photographed Donatello's magnificent life-size sculptures of saints on the high altar of St. Anthony's in Padua, and the great figures of musicians on the portal of the twelfth-century church in Moissac. Now it turned out to provide the only conceivable means (at least the only one I could think of) to be the unseen observer of all sorts of people in public places. I felt like Goya or Daumier rein-carnated when I found in this long lens the pathetic figures of homeless men and women sitting or lying on sidewalks or benches, and odd-looking characters wearing strange getups in the parks.

My 250-millimeter lens proved equally effec-tive for shorter-range intrusions—discovering a romantic couple embracing on a walkway near the Hudson River, observing people resting idly on a bench at Broadway and One-hundredth Street, coming across a hunched woman walk-ing with fixed determination on Fordham Road in the Bronx, peeking at a man and woman shopping on Delancey Street, exploring the city's graffiti-ridden subways. Sometimes I would ask a friend to drive me around so I could be free to let my long lenses roam the urban landscape through the car window to find something totally unexpected, like the man reading a book as he walked along 125th Street.

At the other end of the photographic spec-trum was a pocket 35-millimeter camera I always carry with me on the chance that I will come across a unique opportunity in the course of my everyday life. That is how I caught the sunlight on St. Patrick's Cathedral one after-noon as I was walking up Fifth Avenue to my office, found dusk falling over the buildings in

Harlem as I was driving home one evening, captured an aerial view of the Throgs Neck Bridge as I was coming in for a landing at La Guardia. (Since I am one of those who thinks with his eyes, I always request a window seat on commercial flights, and it is not unusual for me to reach for my pocket camera when a particularly intriguing sight comes into view. Invariably I think how Leonardo da Vinci would have felt if he could have seen just once what we take for granted from the flying machines he so prophetically foresaw.) Other aerial shots, like the ones of downtown Manhattan, I was able to take from a client's helicopter as we made a detour during a business trip.

My passion for sculpture drew my camera eye naturally to details of three-dimensional works of art like the Louise Nevelson on Park Avenue, the Dubuffet at the Chase Manhattan Bank, the Daniel Chester French in front of the Brooklyn Museum, the Saint-Gaudens General Sherman at Fifty-ninth Street and Fifth Avenue, and the Lady on the Fountain in front of the Plaza Hotel. In my books on sculpture I have always made a point of photographing works without people in order to show their pristine forms, but *Our New York* has a different purpose. So I got a special kick out of showing the famous Noguchi Cube as if it were about to fall on an unsuspecting passerby, the World Trade Center sculpture by Nagare as an ideal spot for a souvenir tourist photograph, the pigeon-friendly lion in front of the New York Public Library. And I was delighted to see abstract sculptural forms in the dramatic faces of buildings, details of bridges, lampposts swooping into the sky.

Wall paintings and patinated building exteriors and graffiti fascinate me—the latter especially when there are words that carry a sublime message like "R nation better under God than under Red UN BOSS." I also feel I can make some kind of statement about the city when I get a shot of the Empire State Building through what looks like (but isn't) barbed wire, or of the fantastic gingerbread top of a building near Seventy-second Street and Broadway, which I have passed at least a thousand times but never noticed, or the wonderful sculptured facade of the building on Fifty-eighth Street and Seventh Avenue, which I look at often with admiration.

Central Park is one of my favorite places in the world. It has been with me all my life, and I still drive through it every day on my way to work. As far as I am concerned, there is no place more beautiful on earth than those rocks, trees, meadows, lakes. And so it was a special pleasure for me to try to show how utterly breathtaking those pastoral landscapes are. As I printed the many photographs I took of the park the words kept going through my mind: "Who would ever imagine that these scenes could be found in a park located in the middle of Manhattan!" I hoped the photographs would inspire people to look with a fresh eye the next time they walked along the paths and through the glades of Central Park.

Alfred had the idea that I should photograph some of the leading cultural and intellectual lights of New York, and he went with me to photograph Noguchi, Motherwell, Isaac Bashevis Singer, and my uncle Louis Finkelstein in their homes. My daughter Amy went with me as my assistant when I photographed Gordon Parks (it was quite an experience photographing the photographer!) and Saul Steinberg. She also took the photograph of Alfred and me for the jacket of the book. Later my granddaughter Rachel became my assistant, and she was even one of my subjects when I photographed the

Ken Smyth sculpture on the Battery Park City Esplanade.

Alfred and I met periodically over the years to talk about our experiences in the city, occasionally to visit together places or people who had meant a lot to one or both of us, and sometimes to take photographs of subjects that Alfred was particularly interested in. And as my collection of photographs grew, Alfred and I went over them to discuss the associations they brought to mind. Alfred was always very generous in his comments about the photographs, and once he even invited me to give a lecture to one of his classes at CUNY Graduate School, showing my collection of New York photographs and explaining what they meant to me.

Making the selection of photographs for the book and planning the design was an especially difficult task. Initially I chose one hundred photographs for Alfred to review and then took some more after we talked about them. Alfred had written some of the text while I was taking the photographs, but he did most of the writing later on. Neither of us wanted to feel that we were illustrating or describing the other's work; we just wanted to be on the same wavelength. It was truly a remarkable kind of partnership that worked because we were both lifelong New Yorkers and had much in common. Ultimately it was our editor, Arthur Samuelson, and the designers of the book, Ulrich Ruchti and Michael Schubert, who made the selection of photographs that helped to bring unity to our collaborative effort.

The photographs should not be considered in any way a comprehensive picture of New York. There are many important sites in the city that I did not photograph and that would belong in a more traditional approach to a book on New York. Also, now that my eye has become sensitized to New York images, I am constantly finding new shots I wish I could take to make an even stronger statement about what the city means to me. And yet I am pleased with the result, and gratified that the statements Alfred and I have made in our respective mediums can stand together as a unique personal portrait of our city.

David Finn